Big Yarn, Beautiful Lace Knits

Barbara Benson

STACKPOLE BOOKS

Guilford, Connecticut

Published by Stackpole Books
An imprint of The Rowman & Littlefield Publishing Group, Inc.
4501 Forbes Blvd., Ste. 200
Lanham, MD 20706
www.stackpolebooks.com

Distributed by NATIONAL BOOK NETWORK
800-462-6420

British Library Cataloguing in Publication Information available

Library of Congress Cataloging-in-Publication Data

Names: Benson, Barbara, 1973– author.
Title: Big yarn, beautiful lace knits : 20 shawls, hats, ponchos, and more in
  bulky yarn / Barbara Benson.
Description: First edition. | Guilford, Connecticut : Stackpole Books, 2019.
  Identifiers: LCCN 2018052419 (print) | LCCN 2018054191 (ebook) | ISBN
  9780811767804 (electronic) | ISBN 9780811737876 (pbk. : alk. paper)
Subjects: LCSH: Knitting. | Knitting—Patterns. | Yarn.
Classification: LCC TT820 (ebook) | LCC TT820 .B49 2019 (print) | DDC
  746.43/2—dc23
LC record available at https://lccn.loc.gov/2018052419

♾™ The paper used in this publication meets the minimum requirements of American National Standard for Information Sciences—Permanence of Paper for Printed Library Materials, ANSI/NISO Z39.48-1992.

First Edition

Printed in the United States of America

∞ CONTENTS ∞

Introduction v

Getting Started with Lace 1

The Patterns 7

Shoot the Moon. 9
Asymmetrical Balance. 13
Sparrow Grass Hat 17
Rocinante 23
Coefficient of Modulation 27
To Warmly Go 31
Giant Elves 37
Teeter Totter Toque 41
Cinches and Ladders 45
Signet Throw 49

Dash Panel .55
Un, Deux, Trois. 59
Bonus Stitch Hat 65
Drunk Spider 69
Shorty Squiggle Mitts 73
Hearts in Chains Poncho 77
Rupee Slouch. 83
Avasarala 89
Bitis Shawl .95
Iguazu Falls 101

Techniques 107

Knitting in the Round. 108
Cast-On/Bind-Off. 109

Abbreviations 115
Yarn Sources 119
Acknowledgments 120
Visual Index 121

∞ INTRODUCTION ∞

The word "lace" when used in conjunction with the word "knitting" evokes images of a delicate filigree of holes scattered across a field of fabric made up of fine yarn. In the Orenburg knitting tradition there are even shawls known as wedding ring shawls because they are knit of such delicate yarn the entire shawl can be drawn through a wedding ring. I love this type of lace and have knit many projects using lightweight yarn in ornate lace patterns.

However, there is something in me that always goads me in the direction of the notorious "What if?": *What if I did this differently?* In my first book, *Mosaic & Lace Knits: 20 Innovative Patterns Combining Slip-Stitch Colorwork and Lace Techniques* (2017), the result of asking "What if?" was combining colorwork, which is traditionally regarded as a dense, warm fabric, with the open airiness of lace. As I further pondered lace, I started wondering what these beautiful patterns would look like writ large. I started asking myself: *If instead of fine yarns I used heavier, even bulky yarns, what would that look like?*

The answer is found in the pages of this book! By exploring a wide assortment of bulky and chunky yarns, I developed a collection of projects that range from bold and graphic to patterns that somehow maintain their delicate appearance despite their heft. And, of course, since they are worked in big yarn, with even bigger needles, they knit up much more quickly than their lightweight yarn counterparts.

While developing the patterns in this book, I have learned that not all lace patterns play well with all yarns. My experimentation has shown that smaller motifs take on bold new looks when knit in bulky yarn, simple mesh magnifies into impressive panels of pop art, and double yarn overs create an airy effect that lightens up even the heaviest of yarns. It has been a fun learning process, and I look forward to sharing it with you.

Getting Started with Lace

What Is Lace?

At its most basic, lace is making holes in your knitting on purpose. When you make a hole with a yarn over, you have added a stitch to your stitch count. Therefore, unless you want to increase your stitch count, you need to pair the yarn over with a decrease to return your stitch count to its original number. When pairings of increases (yarn overs) and decreases are arranged in attractive patterns, the end result is lace! A further refinement of this explanation includes knitted lace versus lace knitting. "Lace knitting" is the term used when all of the yarn overs and their paired decreases are confined to one side of your knitting, typically the right side. The return row, usually the wrong side, is then simply knitted or purled. "Knitted lace," by contrast, is the term used when yarn overs and decreases are found on both sides of your knitting; there are no "rest" rows.

Reading a Chart

SYMBOLS

A traditional knitting chart illustrates what the finished stitch pattern will look like if viewed from the right side of the fabric. The symbols that represent the stitches are also depicted as they appear from the right side. Therefore, when you are knitting back and forth in rows, an empty box represents a knit stitch when working on the right side, but it represents a purl stitch when working on the wrong side. Always consult the stitch legend for each pattern and familiarize yourself with what each symbol means before you start knitting.

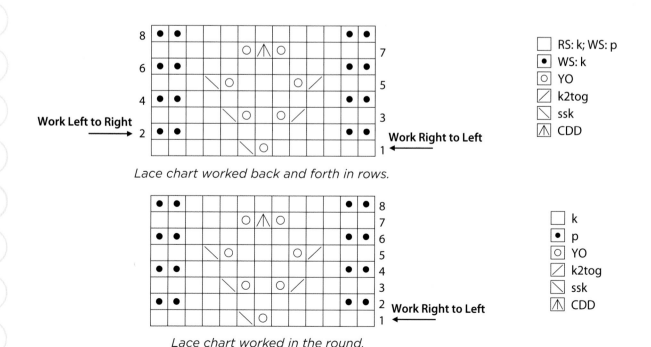

Lace chart worked back and forth in rows.

Lace chart worked in the round.

DIRECTIONALITY

To read a chart, always start reading a row or round where the number for that row or round is located. Row 1 will usually be located in the bottom right, but not always. Right-side rows are read from right to left; wrong-side rows are read from left to right. Work each stitch as indicated by the symbol as defined in the stitch legend. If you are working back and forth in rows, you will read the next row in the opposite direction from the row below. If you are working in the round, you will read every round from right to left. Proceed in this manner until you have completed the chart as instructed by the pattern.

REPEATS

There are frequently marked sections of a chart that are repeated across a row or round. These portions will be highlighted with a repeat box that defines the edges of the repeat. Always refer to the instructions to determine how many times you will need to repeat the indicated stitches. Often repeated sections fall between groups of stitches that do not repeat. Pay careful attention to how many non-repeated stitches surround the repeated sections, as they will help you understand how many times the repeated sections are worked. The Drunk Spider cowlette (see page 69) is a good example of repeats framing a section of non-repeated stitches.

NO STITCH

At times the number of increases and decreases do not balance across a row or round or shaping creates extra stitches in a row or round. When this happens, it is necessary to use a "no stitch" symbol in the chart. These symbols help to keep motifs and patterns lined up so you can better compare your knitting to the chart. The no stitch is represented by a gray box and is simply a placeholder. It is exactly what it says—not a stitch. It is telling you that a stitch is missing on the row or round you are working.

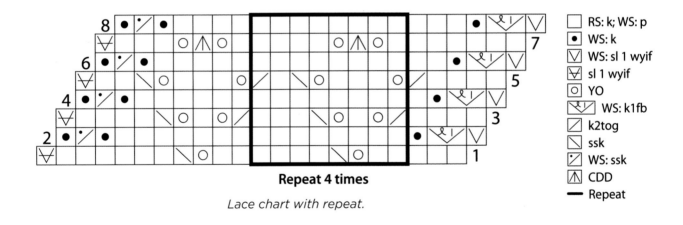

Repeat 4 times

Lace chart with repeat.

	RS: k; WS: p
•	WS: k
V	WS: sl 1 wyif
⩛	sl 1 wyif
O	YO
⩔	WS: k1fb
╱	k2tog
╲	ssk
⟋	WS: ssk
⋀	CDD
▬	Repeat

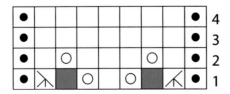

Lace chart with no stitch.

	No stitch
□	k
•	p
O	YO
⋌	sl 1-k2tog-psso
⋋	ssk-pssf-sl 1

On Stitch Markers and Borrowed Stitches

USING STITCH MARKERS

Some of the patterns in this book use stitch markers as waypoints to help you keep track of where you are in the pattern. They are useful tools that can also be beautiful, so have fun with them. Many lace knitters choose to use additional stitch markers between repeats to make sure they have the correct number of stitches in each repeat. If you decide to add markers in this way, I recommend that they be distinctly different from the markers I instruct you to place for shaping or construction in the pattern. This will ensure that you don't get confused.

BORROWED STITCHES

If you choose to add stitch markers to mark repeats, beware! Sometimes, especially in lace, motifs are interlocked and need to borrow stitches from neighboring repeats. When reading a chart, if a repeat line falls between a decrease and its paired yarn over, it is probably borrowing a stitch. Usually the decrease will sit next to the repeat line when this occurs. When this happens, you will need to shift your stitch marker to compensate. For an example of this situation, look at the lace chart with repeat on page 2. Row 5 illustrates a knit two together and its yarn over that are separated by a repeat line. In this example, when you are one stitch before the marker you would slip that stitch, remove the marker, return the stitch to your left-hand needle, knit two together, replace your marker, and then proceed with the chart.

Holes on Purpose: The Yarn Over

Because the yarn over is the defining element of lace, I wanted to include a quick primer on how it is worked. A yarn over is created by simply passing the yarn over the needle, producing a new stitch. However, how you create a yarn over

is dependent on what stitches are both before and after your yarn over.

KNIT BEFORE, KNIT AFTER

The working yarn begins at the back of the work.
1. Move the yarn to the front of the work by passing it between the needles.
2. Pass the yarn over the right-hand needle to the back.

The working yarn is now in back of the work so that you are ready to knit the next stitch.

KNIT BEFORE, PURL AFTER

The working yarn begins at the back of the work.
1. Move the yarn to the front of the work by passing it between the needles.
2. Pass the yarn over the right-hand needle to the back.
3. Move the yarn to the front of the work by passing it between the needles.

The working yarn is now in front of the work so that you are ready to purl the next stitch.

PURL BEFORE, PURL AFTER

The working yarn begins in the front of the work.
1. Pass the yarn over the right-hand needle.
2. Move the yarn to the front of the work by passing it between the needles.

The working yarn is now in front of the work so that you are ready to purl the next stitch.

PURL BEFORE, KNIT AFTER

The working yarn begins in the front of the work.
1. Pass the yarn over the right-hand needle to the back.

The working yarn is now in back of the work so that you are ready to knit the next stitch.

Your New Best Friend— the Double Yarn Over

Many of the patterns in this book use the double yarn over. I have found that I really like the effect produced by the extra big hole combined with the extra big yarn. But there is a wee trick for working the stitch: When creating a double yarn over on the right side, simply wrap the yarn around the needle like a regular yarn over, but then bring the yarn back to the front under the needle and over again for a second yarn over—easy-peasy. The slightly tricky bit happens on the wrong side. If you tried to simply purl, or knit, both of these yarn overs on the return row or round, one of the stitches would magically disappear. In fact, it would be impossible because of the way this stitch is constructed. Instead, you need to knit one of the stitches and purl the other one. All of the patterns in this book will instruct you to do this, but I thought a heads-up and an explanation might be useful.

Lean Left, SSK versus SKP

Both ssk and skp are left-leaning single decreases and can usually be used interchangeably. You may notice that different patterns in this book call for one or the other (and sometimes both in the same project). I wanted to take a moment to explain why. While knitting for this book, I found that with some of the bulkiest yarns, I simply liked the look of the skp better than the ssk. I know this doesn't make any sense because functionally they are the same thing. The right stitch lays over the left stitch and the working yarn is pulled through both—but something about the combination of yarn, needles, and my style of knitting made these stitches look different on the needles. Perhaps it's because you pull that slipped stitch over versus knitting it; I'm not sure, but, for whatever reason, I noticed it the most with the bulkiest yarns. If you prefer one of these stitches to the other, or they look the same when you execute them, then, by all means, feel free to substitute one for the other.

Big Beautiful Yarn

Unfortunately, yarn companies are not required to adhere to specific standards when they classify the weights of yarns. This is most apparent in the chunky, bulky, and super bulky ranges. I chose yarns based on how they were classified

by the manufacturers, and as you work through the patterns in this book, you will notice a striking range of thicknesses. If you plan on substituting yarn, please take careful note of the weight and yardage listed. Even though the label says "bulky," that doesn't mean that yarn is a great substitute for all other "bulky"-labeled yarns.

Bigger Yarn, Bigger Tools

As you explore the world of bigger yarns, you might need to invest in some new tools and notions. Any stitch markers you use will need to have a larger diameter than your needles so that they will slide along easily as you knit. For weaving in ends, your tapestry needle needs to have an eye large enough to accommodate your yarn. And, of course, you need bigger needles!

As the needles you use become fatter, I encourage you to pay attention to the tips. Many needle manufacturers elongate the tip taper of the larger needle sizes to facilitate your knitting. What I mean by the taper is the sloped distance between the end point and the needle shaft, where the needle reaches its fixed and final diameter. This fixed diameter is what determines the size of each stitch and therefore regulates your gauge. When you are knitting, especially with an elongated taper, it can be easy to fall into the bad habit of knitting on the taper instead of on the needle shaft. When knitting on the taper, your gauge can be irregular, and wonky stitches may result. Make sure you move every stitch up to the shaft of the needle before tensioning the yarn and setting the stitch.

Leave a Little Extra on Your Ends

I don't know about you, but weaving in ends is my *favorite* part of knitting (that's sarcasm). A necessary evil, weaving in ends requires a little extra attention when knitting with bulky yarns. However much yarn you typically leave for weaving in ends, leave a little more for bulky yarn.

Bigger yarn just likes wriggling itself out, so you have to be a bit overzealous with your weaving for it to stay in place. I recommend using the duplicate stitch technique just after you finish the knitting; then block the piece with the ends left untrimmed. This allows the ends some wiggle room to shift without coming undone. Once the blocking is complete, run the tail through the backs of a few more stitches, splitting the stitches so that the yarn holds the tail securely. Only then snip the ends. Experiment to find what works best for you—but I don't think you'll regret leaving a bit of extra yarn to fiddle with.

Blocking Makes It Beautiful

Lace loves blocking. With few exceptions, you simply must block lace for it to look its best. When you complete your lace project, it may look like a hot mess, and you might even wonder why you bothered. This is where blocking comes to the rescue. Proper blocking determines the finished size and appearance of your project, so you will either learn to love it or resign yourself to the process if you want your finished items to resemble the photos in these pages.

The fiber content of your yarn will dictate what blocking process you will use, so you need to consider blocking during the planning stage of your project. If you choose a yarn made of natural fibers, you will want to wet block your finished piece. Animal fibers, plant fibers, and cellulose fibers all respond well to wet blocking. If you prefer to use a synthetic fiber such as acrylic, then you need to use steam and heat to block your project. I have deliberately included both natural and synthetic fibers in the yarn selections for this book to show that both work equally well with lace; they just take different approaches.

WET BLOCKING

Wet blocking works best on natural fibers and will need to be done every time you launder your garment. If you make an error in your blocking, or are unsatisfied with the results, you can always re-soak and try again.

To wet block you will need a basin large enough to fully submerge your finished piece, wool wash, towels or a salad spinner, a blocking surface, and blocking tools such as wires, pins, and a yardstick.

The basic steps of wet blocking are as follows:

1. Soak the finished piece in lukewarm water with wool wash for at least twenty minutes.
2. Gently remove as much water as possible from the piece. You can either roll the piece in a series of towels and press out the water or spin the water out with a salad spinner (my preferred method).
3. Lay the damp piece out on your blocking surface and shape to finished measurements using blocking tools such as wires and pins. Measure with a yardstick. I don't recommend using a measuring tape; because of its flexibility and stretchability, you can make a measuring tape say pretty much whatever you want.
4. Allow the piece to dry completely and then remove from surface.

STEAM HEAT BLOCKING

Steam heat blocking is mainly used for acrylic yarns and only needs to be done once. After blocking your acrylic piece it will stay blocked, but you cannot re-block it to change the effect; you only get one shot. You can also use steam heat blocking on most natural fibers, but this is not the same as steam cleaning them; if you need to launder the piece, you may end up with different results after it has been washed.

To steam heat block, you will need an iron with a steam setting or a hand-held steamer with a high-heat setting. You will also need a blocking surface, blocking tools such as wires and pins, and a yardstick.

The basic steps of steam heat blocking are as follows:

1. Preheat your iron or steamer filled with distilled water.
2. Lay out the piece on your blocking surface and shape to finished measurements using blocking tools such as wires and pins. Measure with a yardstick. I don't recommend using a measuring tape; because of its flexibility and stretchability, you can make a

measuring tape say pretty much whatever you want.

3. Working in small sections, hold the steam source about a half inch above the surface of the knitting and allow the steam and heat to penetrate the fibers for ten to fifteen seconds or until the yarn relaxes. If using an iron, be *very* careful not to touch the hot surface of the iron to the knitting—if you're blocking acrylic, it will melt and ruin the yarn. Continue in this manner, hovering just above overlapping sections of the piece until you have steamed every square inch.

4. After piece is completely cooled and dried, remove the blocking pins while carefully observing how the piece reacts. If you remove a pin and the fabric draws in substantially, stretch it back to the desired location and pin again. Apply additional steam until the fabric stays put—a small amount of retraction is normal, large movement is not.

A Note on Gauge

Even though most of the projects in this book are not what one would consider fitted, gauge is still important. Gauge affects both the drape and the yarn usage of a project. Being off gauge could cause you to have lace that is either too dense or too floppy. More alarmingly, it could also cause you to run out of yarn. When you knit a gauge swatch, be sure to do it with the same needles and using the same techniques that you will use for your project. If you will be knitting back and forth in rows, swatch back and forth in rows. If you will be knitting in the round, swatch in the round. All gauge measurements for the projects in this book are listed for blocked gauge, so be sure to block your gauge swatch using the same technique that you will use for the finished piece.

The Patterns

Shoot the Moon

Sometimes all the lace you need is some simple mesh. The asymmetrical shaping of this piece is exaggerated by the balance of lace to stockinette stitch in the patterning. The result is a piece that can be worn in a variety of different ways. When laid out flat, the solid portion of this shawl forms a crescent moon that appears to be trailing a fine mesh in its wake. That made me wonder whether we could have shooting moons to go with our shooting stars.

Finished Size: 21.75 in. (55 cm) deep and 32 in. (81.5 cm) wingspan

Yarn: Cascade Yarns 128 Superwash (100% superwash merino wool; 128 yd./117 m; 3.5 oz./ 100 g); Turtle, 2 skeins, approximately 226 yd. (207 m)

Needles: US size 11 (8 mm) 40 in. (100 cm) circular needle

Notions: Stitch marker, tapestry needle

Gauge: 12.5 sts and 18 rows = 4 in. (10 cm) in St st, blocked

Special Stitches

k1fb: Knit one front and back; knit into the front loop of the next stitch as usual but leave it on the needle, then knit into the back loop of the same stitch. One stitch increased.

kYOk: Knit, yarn over, knit; knit into the front loop of next stitch as usual but leave it on the needle, YO, then knit into the same stitch again. Two stitches increased.

Note: This shawl is easily adjustable. I worked seven repeats of the body pattern, but you could easily keep going until you have just enough yarn for binding off (a tail about three times the length of the bind-off edge).

Instructions

Using the Long Tail Cast-On method (see page 111), CO 3 sts.

(see page 111)

SET-UP

Row 1 (RS): K1, YO, k2—4 sts.

Row 2 (WS): Sl 1 wyif, k2, sl 1 wyif.

Row 3: K1, kYOk, k2—6 sts.

Row 4: Sl 1 wyif, k1, p1, k1fb, k1, sl 1 wyif—7 sts.

Row 5: K1, kYOk, k5—9 sts.

Row 6: Sl 1 wyif, k1, p4, k1fb, k1, sl 1 wyif—10 sts.

Row 7: K1, kYOk, k3, k2tog, YO, k1, ssk—11 sts.

Row 8: Sl 1 wyif, k1, p6, k1fb, k1, sl 1 wyif—12 sts.

Row 9: K1, kYOk, k3, (k2tog, YO) twice, k1, ssk—13 sts.

Row 10: Sl 1 wyif, k1, p8, k1fb, k1, sl 1 wyif—14 sts.

Row 11: K1, kYOk, k3, pm, (k2tog, YO) 3 times, k1, ssk—15 sts.

Row 12: Sl 1 wyif, k1, p10, k1fb, k1, sl 1 wyif—16 sts.

Modify Me!

This shawl can easily be made larger or smaller just by working more or fewer repeats than indicated. You can also knit it in a different yarn weight, but you'll need to change your needle size and yarn amount accordingly.

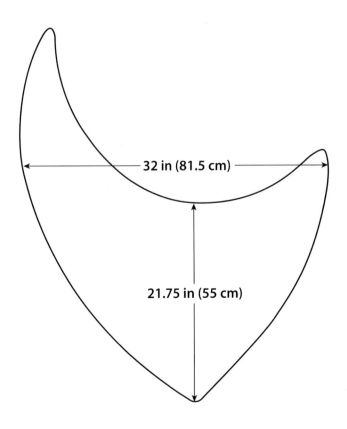

BODY

Row 1: K1, kYOk, knit to 1 st before m, sl 1, rm, return sl st to LH needle, pm on RH needle, *k2tog, YO; rep from * to last 3 sts, k1, ssk—1 st inc'd.

Row 2: Sl 1 wyif, k1, purl to last 3 sts, k1fb, k1, sl 1 wyif—1 st inc'd.

Rows 3–6: Rep Rows 1 and 2 twice—4 sts inc'd.

Row 7: K1, kYOk, knit to 3 sts before m, sl 3, rm, return sl sts to LH needle, pm on RH needle, *k2tog, YO; rep from * to last 3 sts, k1, ssk—1 st inc'd.

Row 8: Sl 1 wyif, k1, purl to last 3 sts, k1fb, k1, sl 1 wyif—1 st inc'd.

Rows 9–12: Rep Rows 7 and 8 twice—4 sts inc'd.

Rep Rows 1–12 six more times—100 sts.

FINISHING

Using the Expandable Lace Bind-Off, Knit Variant method (see page 112), BO all sts.

Weave in ends. Wet block to measurements. Trim ends.

32 in (81.5 cm)

21.75 in (55 cm)

Asymmetrical Balance

Far from ornate, the lace in this deeply smooshy scarf presents a crisp, asymmetrical balance featuring double yarn overs. One challenge that I am forever wrestling with is designing lace patterns that your average man can also wear. Lace is typically perceived as feminine, but when combined with bulky yarns and streamlined features, I think I might just have met this challenge.

Finished Size: 7 in. (17.75 cm) wide, 84 in. (213.5 cm) long

Yarn: Berroco Catena (94% extra-fine merino wool, 6% nylon; 120 yd./110 m; 1.75 oz./50 g); Citrine, 3 skeins, approximately 310 yd. (283 m)

Needles: US size 11 (8 mm)

Notions: Tapestry needle

Gauge: 19 sts and 19 rows = 4 in. (10 cm) in k1, p1 ribbing

Instructions

Using the Long Tail Cast-On method (see page 111), CO 28 sts.

Set-Up Row (WS): Sl 2 wyif, p2, (k1, p1) 5 times, k1, p8, k1, p2, sl 2 wyif.

BODY

Row 1 (RS): K4, p1, k2, k2tog, YO twice, ssk, k2, (p1, k1) 6 times, k3.

Row 2 (WS): Sl 2 wyif, p2, (k1, p1) 6 times, p2, k1, p4, k1, p2, sl 2 wyif.

Row 3: K4, p1, (k2tog, YO twice, ssk) twice, (p1, k1) 6 times, k3.

Row 4: Sl 2 wyif, p2, (k1, p1) 7 times, p2, (k1, p2) twice, sl 2 wyif.

Rep Rows 1–4 eighty-eight more times or until scarf is desired length, then work Rows 1 and 2 once more.

Next Row: K4, p1, k8, (p1, k1) 6 times, k3.

Bind off from the WS as follows: Sl 2 wyif, insert LH needle through front loops of last 2 sts on RH needle and k2tog tbl, p1, with yarn in front sl both sts back to the LH needle pwise, p2tog, (p1, with yarn in front sl last 2 sts back to the LH needle pwise, p2tog, k1, lift right-most st on RH needle up, over, and off the tip of the needle) 6 times, (p1, with yarn in front sl last 2 sts back to the LH needle pwise, p2tog) 8 times, k1, lift right-most st on RH needle up, over, and off the tip of the needle, (p1, with yarn in front sl last 2 sts back to the LH needle pwise, p2tog) twice, sl 2 wyif, with yarn in front sl last 3 sts back to the LH needle pwise, p3tog.

FINISHING

Weave in ends. Wet block to open lace but leave ribbing compressed. Trim ends.

Modify Me!
If you'd like a cowl instead of a scarf, you can work fewer pattern repeats, and then either seam or button the ends together. Maybe even try giving it a twist to make a faux Mobius!

Sparrow Grass Hat

When you twist a stitch, that stitch positively pops off of the fabric. Combine this effect with lace, and magical things happen. I decided that this motif looked like the tips of asparagus, but asparagus is not very poetic. Luckily, I discovered that the folk name for this spring vegetable is sparrow grass, which has a lovely ring to it, don't you think?

Finished Size: 17.75 in. (45 cm) brim circumference, 8.75 in. (22 cm) tall

Yarn: Knit Picks Wool of the Andes™ Superwash Bulky (100% wool; 137 yd./125 m; 3.5 oz./100 g); Oyster Heather, 1 skein, approximately 92 yd. (84 m)

Needles: *Brim:* US size 9 (5.5 mm) 16 in. (40 cm) circular needle; *Body:* US size 10 (6 mm) 16 in. (40 cm) circular needle and set of dpns or your choice of small-circumference knitting needles (see Knitting in the Round, page 108)

Notions: Stitch marker, tapestry needle

Gauge: 18 sts and 21 rows = 4 in. (10 cm) in Twisted Ribbing in the rnd on larger needle, blocked

Special Stitches

sl 1-k2tog-psso: Slip one, knit two together, pass slipped stitch over; slip one stitch as to knit, knit the next two stitches together as one, insert left-hand needle into the front loop of the slipped stitch from left to right and pass it over the k2tog stitch and drop it off the needle. Two stitches decreased.

ssk-pssf-sl 1: Slip, slip, knit, pass slipped stitch forward, slip; ssk, then return new stitch to left-hand needle, pass the second stitch on left-hand needle over the ssk stitch and off the needle, slip ssk stitch purlwise back to right-hand needle. Two stitches decreased.

Stitch Guide

TWISTED RIBBING
Rnd 1: *K1 tbl, p1; rep from * to EOR.
Rep Rnd 1 for pattern.

BODY CHART WRITTEN INSTRUCTIONS

Note: The st count decreases to 72 sts on Rnd 1 and returns to 80 on Rnd 2.

Rnd 1: [(K1 tbl, p1) 6 times, ssk-pssf-sl 1, YO, k1, YO, sl 1-k2tog-psso, p1] 4 times—72 sts.
Rnd 2: [(K1 tbl, p1) 6 times, k1, YO, k3, YO, k1, p1] 4 times—80 sts.
Rnds 3 and 4: [(K1 tbl, p1) 6 times, k7, p1] 4 times.
Rep Rnds 1–4 for pattern.

TRANSITION CHART WRITTEN INSTRUCTIONS

Note: The st count decreases to 72 sts on Rnds 1 and 5 and returns to 80 on Rnds 2 and 6.

Rnd 1: (K1 tbl, p1, ssk-pssf-sl 1, YO, k1, YO, sl 1-k2tog-psso, p1, k1 tbl, p1, YO, ssk, k3, k2tog, YO, p1) 4 times—72 sts.
Rnd 2: (K1 tbl, p1, k1, YO, k3, YO, k1, p1, k1 tbl, p1, k7, p1) 4 times—80 sts.
Rnd 3: (K1 tbl, p1, k7, p1, k1 tbl, p1, k1, YO, ssk, k1, k2tog, YO, k1, p1) 4 times.
Rnd 4: [K1 tbl, p1, k7, (p1, k1 tbl) twice, k5, k1 tbl, p1] 4 times.
Rnd 5: [K1 tbl, p1, ssk-pssf-sl 1, YO, k1, YO, sl 1-k2tog-psso, (p1, k1 tbl) twice, p1, YO, sl 1-k2tog-psso, YO, p1, k1 tbl, p1] 4 times—72 sts.
Rnd 6: [K1 tbl, p1, k1, YO, k3, YO, k1, (p1, k1 tbl) twice, p1, k3, p1, k1 tbl, p1] 4 times—80 sts.
Rnds 7 and 8: [K1 tbl, p1, k7, (p1, k1 tbl) 5 times, p1] 4 times.

CROWN CHART WRITTEN INSTRUCTIONS
Rnd 1: [K1 tbl, p1, ssk-pssf-sl 1, YO, k1, YO, sl 1-k2tog-psso, (p1, k1 tbl) twice, p1, sl 1-k2tog-psso, p1, k1 tbl, p1] 4 times—64 sts.

Rnd 2: [K1 tbl, p1, k1, YO, k3, YO, k1, (p1, k1 tbl) 4 times, p1] 4 times—72 sts.
Rnd 3: [K1 tbl, p1, k7, (p1, k1 tbl) twice, sl 1-k2tog-psso, k1 tbl, p1] 4 times—64 sts.
Rnd 4: [K1 tbl, p1, k7, (p1, k1 tbl) 3 times, p1] 4 times.
Rnd 5: (K1 tbl, p1, ssk-pssf-sl 1, YO, k1, YO, sl 1-k2tog-psso, p1, k1 tbl, p1, sl 1-k2tog-psso, p1) 4 times—48 sts.
Rnd 6: [K1 tbl, p1, k1, YO, k3, YO, k1, (p1, k1 tbl) twice, p1] 4 times—56 sts.
Rnd 7: (K1 tbl, p1, k7, p1, k1 tbl, sl 1-k2tog-psso) 4 times—48 sts.
Rnd 8: (K1 tbl, p1, k7, p1, k1 tbl, p1) 4 times.
Rnd 9: (Ssk, YO, ssk, k3, k2tog, YO, k2tog, p1) 4 times—40 sts.
Rnd 10: (K1 tbl, k7, k1 tbl, p1) 4 times.
Rnd 11: (Ssk, YO, ssk, k1, k2tog, YO, k2tog, p1) 4 times—32 sts.
Rnd 12: (K1 tbl, k5, k1 tbl, p1) 4 times.
Rnd 13: (Ssk, YO, sl 1-k2tog-psso, YO, k2tog, p1) 4 times—24 sts.
Rnd 14: (K1 tbl, k3, k1 tbl, p1) 4 times.
Rnd 15: (Ssk, p1, k2tog, p1) 4 times—16 sts.
Rnd 16: (K1 tbl, p1) 8 times.
Rnd 17: (Sl 1-k2tog-psso, p1) 4 times—8 sts.

Instructions

Using smaller needle and the Long Tail Cast-On method (see page 111), CO 80 sts. Pm to indicate EOR and join to work in the rnd, being careful not to twist sts.

BRIM
Work Twisted Ribbing for 4 rnds. (See Stitch Guide at left for Twisted Ribbing.)

BODY
Switch to larger needle.

Work Body Chart Rnds 1–4 four times, working chart 4 times around each rnd. (See Stitch Guide at left for written chart instructions.)

Work Transition Chart Rnds 1–8 once, working chart 4 times around each rnd. (See Stitch Guide at left for written chart instructions.)

Work Crown Chart Rnds 1–17 once, working chart 4 times around each rnd and switching to dpns or your preferred small-circumference knitting method when the number of sts gets too small for the 16 in. (40 cm) needle. (See Stitch Guide at left for written chart instructions.)

Body Chart

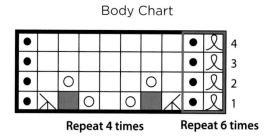

Repeat 4 times   **Repeat 6 times**

Transition Chart

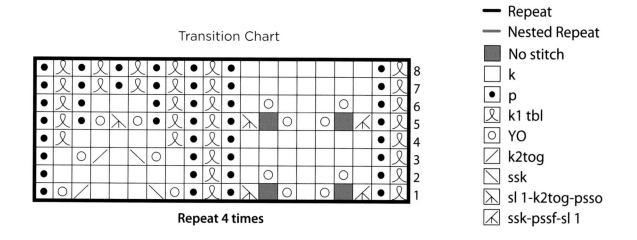

Repeat 4 times

— Repeat
— Nested Repeat
▨ No stitch
☐ k
• p
Ɽ k1 tbl
○ YO
╱ k2tog
╲ ssk
⅄ sl 1-k2tog-psso
⅄ ssk-pssf-sl 1

Crown Chart

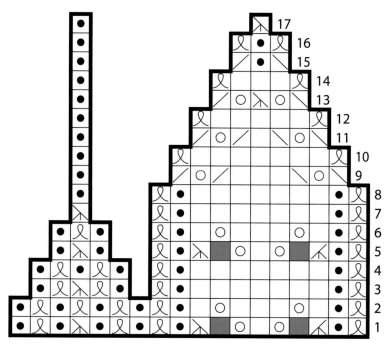

Repeat 4 times

FINISHING

Break yarn leaving a 7 in. (18 cm) tail.

Thread tail onto tapestry needle and pull through remaining sts. Pull tail to cinch closed.

Weave in ends. Wet block over bowl or balloon, being careful to not stretch the ribbing. Trim ends.

Modify Me!

I chose to give this hat a short brim. If you'd like a larger one, simply work more rounds of the twisted ribbing before beginning the body. You can even make it long enough to have a fold-over brim!

Rocinante

There has been a recent resurgence in the popularity of ponchos, and I think it's great! With the proliferation in poncho fashion has come an explosion of poncho constructions. Rocinante uses one of the easiest ways to create one of these carefree accessories. Simply knit a rectangle, sew the short end to the side of the long end, and then poof: poncho! To make the most of the lace, be sure to block it before you seam.

Finished Size: 16 in. (40.5 cm) wide, 53 in. (134.5 cm) long (flat)

Yarn: Spud & Chloë Outer (65% wool, 35% organic cotton; 60 yd./55 m; 3.5 oz./100 g); Sequoia #720500, 4 skeins, approximately 215 yd. (197 m)

Needles: US size 15 (10 mm)

Notions: Tapestry needle

Gauge: 8 sts and 12 rows = 4 in. (10 cm) in St st, blocked; 8 sts and 10 rows = 4 in. (10 cm) in Lace Pattern, blocked

Note

- The pattern as written creates a neck opening that is approximately 32 in. (81.25 cm) in circumference. If you are making the poncho for a smaller individual, you can omit repeats from the length. Each repeat omitted will remove slightly more than 3 in. (7.5 cm) from the neck opening.

Special Stitches

CDD: Central double decrease; slip two stitches as if to k2tog, knit next stitch, and pass both slipped stitches over together. Two stitches decreased.

Stitch Guide

CHART WRITTEN INSTRUCTIONS

Row 1 (RS): K1, (k1, YO, k3, CDD, k3, YO) 3 times, k1, sl 1 wyif—33 sts.

Row 2 (WS): K2, (p9, k1) 3 times, sl 1 wyif.

Row 3: K1, (p2, YO, k2, CDD, k2, YO, p1) 3 times, p1, sl 1 wyif.

Row 4: K2, (k1, p7, k2) 3 times, sl 1 wyif.

Row 5: K1, (p3, YO, k1, CDD, k1, YO, p2) 3 times, p1, sl 1 wyif.

Row 6: K2, (k2, p5, k3) 3 times, sl 1 wyif.

Row 7: K1, (p4, YO, CDD, YO, p3) 3 times, p1, sl 1 wyif.

Row 8: K1, purl to last st, sl 1 wyif.

Rep Rows 1–8 for pattern.

Chart

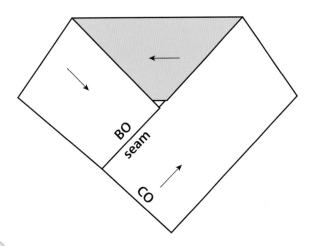

Repeat 3 times

- ▬ Repeat
- ☐ RS: k; WS: p
- ● RS: p; WS: k
- ☑ WS: sl 1 wyif
- ☒ sl 1 wyif
- ⊙ YO
- ⋀ CDD

Instructions

Using the Long Tail Cast-On method (see page 111), CO 33 sts.

Set-Up Row (WS): K2, purl to last 2 sts, k1, sl 1 wyif.

Work Chart Rows 1–8 seventeen times, working rep section 3 times. (See Stitch Guide at left for written chart instructions.)

Using the Expandable Lace Bind-Off, Knit Variant method (see page 112), BO all sts.

FINISHING

Weave in ends. Wet block to finished measurements. Seam bound-off edge to side of left side of rectangle, aligning left side to cast-on edge (see schematic at bottom left). Weave in and trim ends.

Coefficient of Modulation

The subject of my first book was mosaic lace, a combination of slip-stitch colorwork and lace techniques, and I couldn't resist including a mosaic lace pattern in this book. The separation of the increases from their paired decreases creates a wonderful wave pattern that undulates along the entire length of this cowl. The thought of wave forms sent me searching for mathematical wave terminology, which ultimately led to the scientific-sounding name of this piece.

Finished Size: 76.75 in. (195 cm) in circumference, 5 in. (12.5 cm) wide

Yarn: Stitch Sprouts Crater Lake (100% superwash merino wool; 110 yd./101 m; 3.5 oz./ 100 g); Old Man (A), Skell (B), 1 skein each, approximately 85 yd. (78 m) each

Needles: US size 11 (8 mm) 47 in. (119 cm) circular needle (see Knitting in the Round, page 108)

Notions: Stitch marker, tapestry needle

Gauge: 12 sts and 16 rows = 4 in. (10 cm) in St st in the rnd, blocked; 12.5 sts and 19 rows = 4 in. (10 cm) in Lace Pattern in the rnd, blocked

Note
- The stitch count increases to 240 on Round 1 and returns to 220 on Round 3.

Modify Me!

This cowl has a 22-stitch repeat. If you cast on fewer stitches, subtracting in groups of twenty-two, you can make a cowl that will fit closer to the neck. Should you do this, you'll probably also want to work more vertical repeats to make it taller!

Stitch Guide

CHART WRITTEN INSTRUCTIONS

Rnd 1: With A, [sl 1, k1, k2tog, (sl 1, k1) 3 times, (YO, k1) 4 times, (sl 1, k1) twice, sl 1, ssk, k1] 10 times—240 sts.

Rnd 2: With A, [sl 1, k2, (sl 1, k1) 3 times, k8, (sl 1, k1) 3 times, k1] 10 times.

Rnd 3: With B, [k1, k2tog, (k1, sl 1) 3 times, k7, (sl 1, k1) 3 times, ssk] 10 times—220 sts.

Rnd 4: With B, [k2, (k1, sl 1) 3 times, k7, (sl 1 k1) 3 times, k1] 10 times.

Rep Rnds 1–4 for pattern.

Instructions

Using Color B and the Cable Cast-On method (see page 109), CO 220 sts. Pm to indicate EOR and join to work in the rnd, being careful not to twist sts.

SET-UP

Rnd 1: Knit.

Rnd 2: Purl.

BODY

Work Chart Rnds 1–4 four times, working chart 10 times around each rnd, then work Rnd 1 once more, working chart 10 times around—240 sts. (See Stitch Guide above for written chart instructions.)

END

Rnd 1: With A, [sl 1, k2tog, (sl 1, k1) twice, sl 1, k9, (sl 1, k1) twice, sl 1, ssk] 10 times—220 sts.

Rnd 2: With B, knit.

Rnd 3: With B, purl.

Using the Expandable Lace Bind-Off, Knit Variant method (see page 112), BO all sts.

FINISHING

Weave in ends. Wet block to finished measurements pinning points to create a wavy edge. Trim ends.

Chart

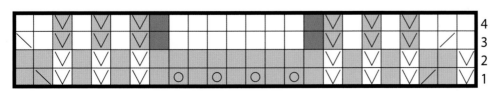

Repeat 10 times

	No stitch
	k
∨	sl 1
○	YO
╱	k2tog
╲	ssk
	Color A
	Color B
—	Repeat

To Warmly Go

As I was knitting the swooping half arch motifs in To Warmly Go, I couldn't help but think of the communicator badges featured in a certain popular science fiction media franchise. Luckily, I can indulge myself in the naming process for my patterns. Originally, I was going to have the motif face the same way on both mitts. However, I found that the lace looked much better reflected. So, I put in the extra time to reflect the charts and made these mitts fraternal twins.

Sizes: S (M, L)

Finished Size: 6.75 (7.25, 8) in. [17 (18.5, 20.5) cm] hand circumference; 11.5 in. (29.25 cm) long

Yarn: Berroco Ultra Alpaca Chunky (50% super fine alpaca, 50% Peruvian wool; 131 yd./ 120 m; 3.5 oz./100 g); Lunar Mix, 1 skein, approximately 83 yd. (76 m)

Needles: US size 10 (6 mm) set of dpns or your choice of small-circumference knitting needles (see Knitting in the Round, page 108)

Notions: 3 stitch markers, tapestry needle

Gauge: 12 sts and 20 rows = 4 in. (10 cm) in St st in the rnd, blocked

Special Stitches

sl 1-k2tog-psso: Slip one, knit two together, pass slipped stitch over; slip one stitch as to knit, knit the next two stitches together as one, insert left-hand needle into the front loop of the slipped stitch from left to right and pass it over the k2tog stitch and drop it off the needle. Two stitches decreased.

ssk-pssf-sl 1: Slip, slip, knit, pass slipped stitch forward, slip; ssk, then return new stitch to left-hand needle, pass the second stitch on left-hand needle over the ssk stitch and off the needle, slip ssk stitch purlwise back to right-hand needle. Two stitches decreased.

Rnd 14: P1, k6, p4.
Rnd 15: P1, ssk, YO, k1, YO, sl 1-k2tog-psso, YO, p4.
Rnd 16: P1, k5, p5.

HALF ARCH LEFT CHART
WRITTEN INSTRUCTIONS
(worked over 11 sts and 16 rnds)
Rnd 1: P4, k2tog, YO, k2, YO, k2tog, p1.
Rnd 2: P4, k6, p1.
Rnd 3: P3, k2tog, YO, k3, YO, k2tog, p1.
Rnd 4: P3, k7, p1.
Rnd 5: P2, k2tog, YO, k4, YO, k2tog, p1.
Rnd 6: P2, k8, p1.
Rnd 7: P1, k2tog, YO, k5, YO, k2tog, p1.
Rnd 8: P1, k9, p1.
Rnd 9: P1, YO, ssk, YO, k1, ssk-pssf-sl 1, k1, YO, k2tog, YO, p1.
Rnd 10: P2, k8, p1.
Rnd 11: P2, YO, ssk, YO, ssk-pssf-sl 1, YO, k2tog, YO, k1, p1.
Rnd 12: P3, k7, p1.
Rnd 13: P3, YO, ssk, k1, k2tog, YO, k2, p1.
Rnd 14: P4, k6, p1.
Rnd 15: P4, YO, ssk-pssf-sl 1, YO, k1, YO, k2tog, p1.
Rnd 16: P5, k5, p1.

RIBBING
Rnd 1: *P1, k1; rep from * to EOR.
Rep Rnd 1 for pattern.

Stitch Guide

HALF ARCH RIGHT CHART
WRITTEN INSTRUCTIONS
(worked over 11 sts and 16 rnds)
Rnd 1: P1, ssk, YO, k2, YO, ssk, p4.
Rnd 2: P1, k6, p4.
Rnd 3: P1, ssk, YO, k3, YO, ssk, p3.
Rnd 4: P1, k7, p3.
Rnd 5: P1, ssk, YO, k4, YO, ssk, p2.
Rnd 6: P1, k8, p2.
Rnd 7: P1, ssk, YO, k5, YO, ssk, p1.
Rnd 8: P1, k9, p1.
Rnd 9: P1, YO, ssk, YO, k1, sl 1-k2tog-psso, k1, YO, k2tog, YO, p1.
Rnd 10: P1, k8, p2.
Rnd 11: P1, k1, YO, ssk, YO, sl 1-k2tog-psso, YO, k2tog, YO, p2.
Rnd 12: P1, k7, p3.
Rnd 13: P1, k2, YO, ssk, k1, k2tog, YO, p3.

Instructions

Using the Long Tail Cast-On method (see page 111), CO 20 (22, 24) sts. Pm to indicate EOR and join to work in the rnd, being careful not to twist sts.

SET-UP
Work 3 rnds of Ribbing (see Stitch Guide above).

RIGHT HAND
Rnd 1: Work Half Arch Right, pm, knit to EOR (these are the palm sts).

Rep Rnd 1 (slipping marker) working Rnds 2–16 of Half Arch Right once, then Rnds 1–7 of Half Arch Right once more.

Thumb Gusset

Continue working chart as established.

Rnd 1: Work Half Arch Right to m, sl m, M1R, pm, knit to EOR—21 (23, 25) sts.

Rnd 2: Work Half Arch Right to m, sl m, k1, sl m, knit to EOR.

Rnd 3: Work Half Arch Right to m, sl m, M1L, knit to m, M1R, sl m, knit to EOR—23 (25, 27) sts.

Rnd 4: Work Half Arch Right to m, sl m, knit to m, sl m, knit to EOR.

Rnd 5: Work Half Arch Right to m, sl m, M1L, knit to m, M1R, sl m, knit to EOR—25 (27, 29) sts.

Rnds 6 and 7: Work Half Arch Right to m, sl m, knit to m, sl m, knit to EOR.

Rep Rnds 5–7 once—27 (29, 31) sts.

Rep Rnds 3 and 4 once—29 (31, 33) sts.

Next Rnd: Work Half Arch Right to m, sl m, transfer 9 gusset sts to waste yarn, rm, knit to EOR—20 (22, 24) sts.

Next Rnd: Work Half Arch Right, sl m, knit to EOR.

Rep last rnd working Rnds 6–16 of Half Arch Right once.

LEFT HAND

Rnd 1: Work Half Arch Left, pm, knit to the EOR (these are the palm sts).

Rep Rnd 1 (slipping marker) working Rnds 2–16 of Half Arch Left once, then Rnds 1–7 of Half Arch Left once more.

Thumb Gusset

Continue working chart as established.

Rnd 1: M1R, pm, work Half Arch Left, sl m, knit to EOR—21 (23, 25) sts.

Rnd 2: Knit to m, sl m, work Half Arch Left to m, sl m, knit to EOR.

Rnd 3: M1L, knit to m, M1R, sl m, work Half Arch Left to m, sl m, knit to EOR—23 (25, 27) sts.

Rnd 4: Knit to m, sl m, work Half Arch Left to m, sl m, knit to EOR.

Half Arch Right

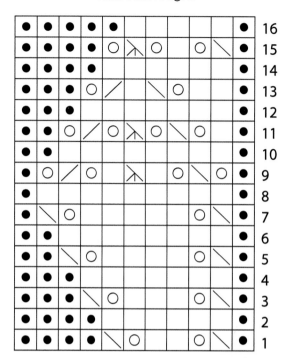

- ☐ k
- ▣ p
- ⊡ YO
- ⊘ k2tog
- ⊠ ssk
- ⊠ ssk-pssf-sl 1
- ⊠ sl 1-k2tog-psso

Half Arch Left

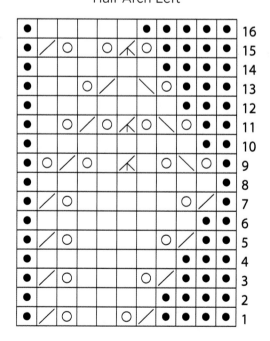

Rnd 5: M1L, knit to m, M1R, sl m, work Half Arch Left to m, sl m, knit to EOR—25 (27, 29) sts.

Rnds 6 and 7: Knit to m, sl m, work Half Arch Left to m, sl m, knit to EOR.

Rep Rnds 5–7 once—27 (29, 31) sts.

Rep Rnds 3 and 4 once—29 (31, 33) sts.

Next Rnd: Transfer 9 gusset sts to waste yarn, rm, work Half Arch Left to m, sl m, knit to EOR—20 (22, 24) sts.

Next Rnd: Work Half Arch Left, sl m, knit to EOR.

Rep last rnd working Rnds 6–16 of Half Arch Left once.

BOTH HANDS

Work 1 rnd of Ribbing.

Using the 1x1 Ribbing Bind-Off method (see page 112), BO all sts.

Thumb

Remount 9 Thumb Gusset sts to needle. Pick up and knit 3 sts where the thumb meets the hand, pm to indicate EOR—12 sts.

Knit 3 rnds. Work 2 rnds of Ribbing.

Using the 1x1 Ribbing Bind-Off method (see page 112), BO all sts.

FINISHING

Weave in ends, using tails to neaten joins at the cuff and to close any holes where the thumb meets the hand. Wet block to open lace. Steam out any crease lines where piece was blocked flat. Trim ends.

Giant Elves

Giant Elves is a perfect example of how bulky yarn loves small motifs. The stitch pattern I used is named "Elfin Lace." When worked in a finer yarn, it brings to mind the stereotypical image of tiny elves flitting through a glade. When worked large, it packs a bigger, bolder punch, and it makes me giggle to think of giant elves.

Finished Size: 16.5 in. (42 cm) wide and 74 in. (188 cm) long; 24 in. (61 cm) along the diagonal

Yarn: Patons Shetland Chunky™ (75% acrylic, 25% wool; 148 yd./136 m; 3.5 oz./100 g); Gold, 3 skeins, approximately 373 yd. (341 m)

Needles: US size 13 (9 mm)

Notions: Tapestry needle

Gauge: 9 sts and 14 rows = 4 in. (10 cm) in St st, blocked; 7.5 sts and 14 rows = 4 in. (10 cm) in Lace Pattern, blocked

Special Stitches

CDD: Central double decrease; slip two stitches as if to k2tog, knit next stitch, and pass both slipped stitches over together. Two stitches decreased.

Stitch Guide

CHART WRITTEN INSTRUCTIONS

Row 1 (RS): K3, (k2, YO, ssk, k4) 5 times, k2, sl 1 wyif.

Row 2 (and all WS rows): K1, ssk, k1, purl to last 3 sts, k1, k1fb, sl 1 wyif.

Row 3: K4, (k2tog, YO, k1, YO, ssk, k3) 5 times, k1, sl 1 wyif.

Row 5: K4, k2tog, (YO, k3, YO, ssk, k1, k2tog) 4 times, YO, k3, YO, ssk, k2, sl 1 wyif.

Row 7: K5, (k2, YO, CDD, YO, k3) 5 times, sl 1 wyif.

Row 8: K1, ssk, k1, purl to last 3 sts, k1, k1fb, sl 1 wyif.

Rep Rows 1–8 for pattern.

Instructions

Using the Long Tail Cast-On method (see page 111), CO 46 sts.

Set-Up Row (WS): K1, ssk, k1, purl to last 3 sts, k1, k1fb, sl 1 wyif.

Work Chart Rows 1–8 twenty-five times, working chart rep 4 times across row. Then work Rows 1–6 once more. (See Stitch Guide at left for written chart instructions.)

Next row (RS): K4, k2tog, YO, (k5, YO, CDD, YO) 4 times, k7, sl 1 wyif.
Next row (WS): K1, ssk, k1, purl to last 3 sts, k1, k1fb, sl 1 wyif.

FINISHING

Using the Expandable Lace Bind-Off, Knit Variant method (see page 112), BO all sts.

Weave in ends. Wet block to finished measurements but also apply the steam heat method.

Note: Because the shawl is worked on the bias, the long edges will be parallel and the short edges will be parallel at an angle (see schematic below). Trim ends.

Modify Me!

This shawl has an eight-stitch repeat. You can easily add or subtract stitches in groups of eight to make this piece wider or narrower. One repeat would make a fun scarf, and if you add enough stitches, you could even make a blanket.

Chart

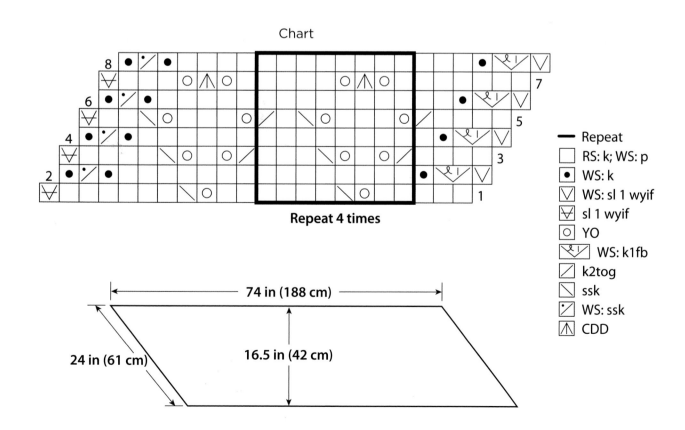

Repeat 4 times

— Repeat
☐ RS: k; WS: p
• WS: k
Ⅴ WS: sl 1 wyif
⩔ sl 1 wyif
○ YO
⤨ WS: k1fb
╱ k2tog
╲ ssk
╱ WS: ssk
⋀ CDD

74 in (188 cm)

24 in (61 cm)

16.5 in (42 cm)

Teeter Totter Toque

In my never-ending quest to do the unexpected, this Teeter Totter Toque is true knitted lace with patterning on every row. But don't let that scare you because you are knitting in the round. This means that all of the wrong-side, purled decreases are actually worked on right-side rounds, which means no purling. Combined with a delicious warm brown acrylic yarn, this is pretty far away from what one might envision as "knitted lace."

Finished Size: 17.5 in. (44.5 cm) around (stretches to 21 in. [53.5 cm] brim circumference) and 9 in. (23 cm) tall

Yarn: Bernat Softee Chunky™ (100% acrylic; 108 yd./99 m; 3.5 oz./100 g); Dark Taupe, 1 skein, approximately 51 yd. (47 m)

Needles: *Brim:* US size 9 (5.5 mm) 16 in. (40 cm) circular needle; *Body:* US size 13 (9 mm) 16 in. (40 cm) circular needle and set of dpns or your choice of small-circumference knitting needles (see Knitting in the Round, page 108)

Notions: Stitch marker, tapestry needle

Gauge: 10 sts and 14 rows = 4 in. (10 cm) in St st in the rnd on larger needle, blocked; 10.5 sts and 13 rows = 4 in. (10 cm) in Lace Pattern in the rnd on larger needle, blocked

Special Stitches

sl 1-k2tog-psso: Slip one, knit two together, pass slipped stitch over; slip one stitch as to knit, knit the next two stitches together as one, insert left-hand needle into the front loop of the slipped stitch from left to right and pass it over the k2tog stitch and drop it off the needle. Two stitches decreased.

ssk-pssf-sl 1: Slip, slip, knit, pass slipped stitch forward, slip; ssk, then return new stitch to left-hand needle, pass the second stitch on left-hand needle over the ssk stitch and off the needle, slip ssk stitch purlwise back to right-hand needle. Two stitches decreased.

Modify Me!

As with Sparrow Grass (page 17), you can give this topper a longer brim by working more rounds of ribbing until it is as long as you desire.

Stitch Guide

CHART WRITTEN INSTRUCTIONS
Rnd 1: (K5, skp, k3, YO, k1, p1) 4 times.
Rnd 2: (K5, skp, k2, YO, k2, p1) 4 times.
Rnd 3: (K5, skp, k1, YO, k3, p1) 4 times.
Rnd 4: (K5, skp, YO, k4, p1) 4 times.
Rnd 5: (K1, YO, k3, k2tog, k5, p1) 4 times.
Rnd 6: (K2, YO, k2, k2tog, k5, p1) 4 times.
Rnd 7: (K3, YO, k1, k2tog, k5, p1) 4 times.
Rnd 8: (K4, YO, k2tog, k5, p1) 4 times.

Rep Rnds 1–8 for pattern.

Instructions

Using smaller needle and the Long Tail Cast-On method (see page 111), CO 48 sts. Pm to indicate EOR and join to work in the rnd, being careful not to twist sts.

BRIM
Ribbing Rnd 1: *K2, p2; rep from * to EOR.

Rep Rnd 1 four more times.

BODY

Work Chart twice, working chart 4 times around each rnd. (See Stitch Guide at left for written chart instructions.)

CROWN

Rnd 1: (K5, sl 1-k2tog-psso, k2, YO, k1, p1) 4 times—44 sts.

Rnd 2: (K5, sl 1-k2tog-psso, k2, p1) 4 times—36 sts.

Rnd 3: (K1, YO, k2, ssk-pssf-sl 1, k2, p1) 4 times—32 sts.

Rnd 4: (K2, ssk-pssf-sl 1, k2, p1) 4 times—24 sts.

Rnd 5: (K2, sl 1-k2tog-psso, YO, p1) 4 times—20 sts.

Rnd 6: (YO, ssk-pssf-sl 1, k1, p1) 4 times—16 sts.

Rnd 7: (K1, sl 1-k2tog-psso) 4 times—8 sts.

FINISHING

Break yarn leaving a 7 in. (18 cm) tail. Thread tail onto a tapestry needle and pull through remaining sts. Pull tail to cinch closed. Weave in ends.

Heat steam block body of hat, but avoid relaxing the ribbing. Fold a hand towel into a dome shape and insert into crown to help steam the decrease portion; then lay hat flat. Steam a small part and then lift the piece and stretch it gently to open lace. Continue working in small sections in this manner until body of hat relaxes and softens.

Chart

						╱	O				8
•						╱		O			7
•						╱			O		6
•						╱				O	5
•					O	╲					4
•				O		╲					3
•			O			╲					2
•		O				╲					1

Repeat 4 times

— Repeat
☐ k
• p
O YO
╱ k2tog
╲ skp

Cinches and Ladders

I cannot resist big, floofy (yes, this is a technical word in knitting) alpaca yarn, but it does present some challenges. The very floofiness that I love fills in the holes in the lace. So, it was go big, or go home! By featuring double yarn overs and a bulky faux-cable, the assertive design elements of Cinches and Ladders stand up to the fuzzy softening of the yarn. The result: you get all of the softness snuggled up against your neck like a kitten, and you get a beautiful lace pattern.

Finished Size: 24 in. (61 cm) around and 14 in. (35.5 cm) tall

Yarn: Plymouth Yarn Baby Alpaca Grande (100% baby alpaca; 110 yd./101 m; 3.5 oz./100 g); #835 Blue Mix, 1 skein, approximately 100 yd. (92 m)

Needles: US size 15 (10 mm) 20 in. (50 cm) circular needle (see Knitting in the Round, page 108)

Notions: Stitch marker, tapestry needle

Gauge: 9 sts and 12 rows = 4 in. (10 cm) in St st in the rnd, blocked; 10 sts and 12 rows = 4 in. (10 cm) in Lace Pattern in the rnd, blocked

Special Stitches

Cinch-4: Sl 1 pwise, k2tog, YO twice, k1, use LH needle to pass sl st over first 4 sts on RH needle and drop off the front of the RH needle.

Stitch Guide

CHART WRITTEN INSTRUCTIONS

Rnd 1: *K2tog, YO twice, ssk, p1, cinch-4, p1; rep from * to EOR.

Rnd 2: *K2, p1, k1, p1; rep from * to EOR.

Rnd 3: *K2tog, YO twice, ssk, p1, k4, p1; rep from * to EOR.

Rnd 4: *K2, p1, k1, p1, k4, p1; rep from * to EOR.

Rep Rnds 1–4 for pattern.

Instructions

Using the Knitted Cast-On method (see page 111), CO 60 sts. Pm to indicate EOR and join to work in the rnd, being careful not to twist sts.

SET-UP

Rnds 1 and 2: *K1, p2, k1, p1; rep from * to EOR.

BODY

Work Chart Rnds 1–4 nine times, working chart 6 times around each rnd. (See Stitch Guide at left for written chart instructions.)

END

Rnd 1: *K2tog, YO twice, ssk, p1, sl 1 pwise, k1, k1fb, k1, use LH needle to pass sl st over first 4 sts on RH needle and drop off the front of the RH needle, p1; rep from * to EOR.

Rnd 2: *K2, p1, k1, p1, k4, p1; rep from * to EOR.

Rnd 3: *K1, p2, k1, p1; rep from * to EOR.

Using the Expandable Lace Bind-Off, Knit Variant method (see page 112), BO all sts.

FINISHING

Weave in ends. Wet block to measurements. Trim ends.

Chart

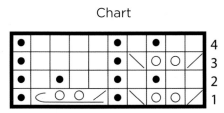

Repeat 6 times

— Repeat

k

• p

|O| YO

k2tog

ssk

cinch-4

Signet Throw

Worked from the center out, this intricate throw reminds me of the coats of arms or symbols sometimes used to represent a family. Your family will love having this throw blanket to ward off just enough of the chill on cool autumn evenings. It will be perfectly at home draped over the back of a couch or across the foot of a bed, bringing an elegant and bold lace statement to any room.

Finished Size: 44 in. (112 cm) wide and 44 in. (112 cm) long

Yarn: Lion Brand Yarns Wool-Ease Thick & Quick (80% acrylic, 20% wool; 106 yd./97 m; 6 oz./170 g); Fisherman, 5 skeins, approximately 520 yd. (476 m)

Note: This pattern uses up more than 90% of the yarn in 5 skeins; if you are not accurate to gauge, you should buy an extra skein.

Needles: US size 13 (9 mm) 47 in. (120 cm) circular needle; optional: US size 13 (9 mm) set of dpns (see Knitting in the Round, page 108)

Notions: 4 stitch markers, 1 different from the others; tapestry needle

Gauge: 10 sts and 12 rows = 4 in. (10 cm) in St st in the rnd, blocked; 8 sts and 14 rows = 4 in. (10 cm) in k2, k1 tbl ribbing, blocked

Note
• Due to the size and complexity of the charts, this pattern does not include written instructions for the lace.

Instructions

Using the Circular Cast-On method (see page 109), CO 8 sts. Pm to indicate EOR and join to work in the rnd, being careful not to twist sts.

SET-UP

Rnd 1: ([K1, YO] twice, pm) 3 times, (k1, YO) twice—16 sts.

Rnd 2: Knit.

Rnd 3: (K1, YO, k3, YO, sl m) 3 times, k1, YO, knit to EOR m, YO—24 sts.

Rnd 4: Knit.

BODY

Work Chart A Rnds 1–28 once, working chart 4 times around each rnd, once between each m—136 sts.

Next, work Eyelet Rnds, as follows:

Eyelet Rnd 1: (K1, M1L, *k2tog, YO; rep from * to 1 st before m, k1, M1R, sl m) 3 times, k1, M1L, *k2tog, YO; rep from * to 1 st before EOR m, k1, M1R—144 sts.

Eyelet Rnd 2: *K1, purl to m, sl m; rep from * 3 times, k1, purl to EOR.

Rep Eyelet Rnds 1 and 2 once—152 sts.

Chart A

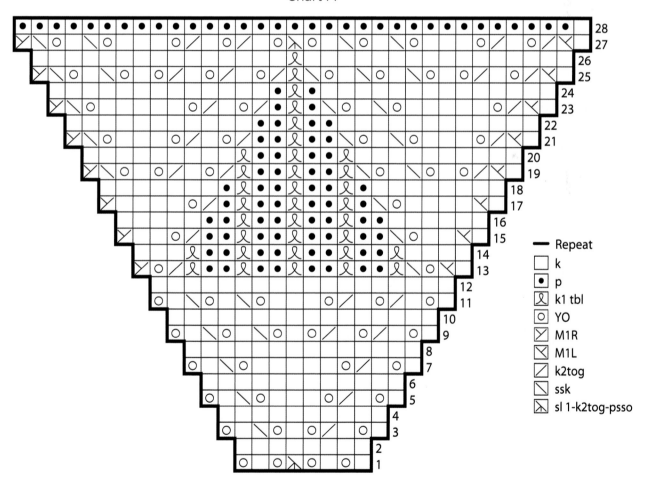

Legend:

— Repeat
☐ k
• p
Ɫ k1 tbl
○ YO
⅄ M1R
⋉ M1L
╱ k2tog
╲ ssk
⋏ sl 1-k2tog-psso

Work Chart B Rnds 1–32 once, working chart 4 times around each rnd, once between each m, marked rep section gets worked twice in each section—208 sts.

END

Work Eyelet Rnds 1 and 2 once, and then work Eyelet Rnd 1 once more—224 sts.

Using the Expandable Lace Bind-Off, Purl Variant method (see page 112), BO all sts.

FINISHING

Weave in ends. Assertively steam heat block to measurements. Trim ends.

Chart B

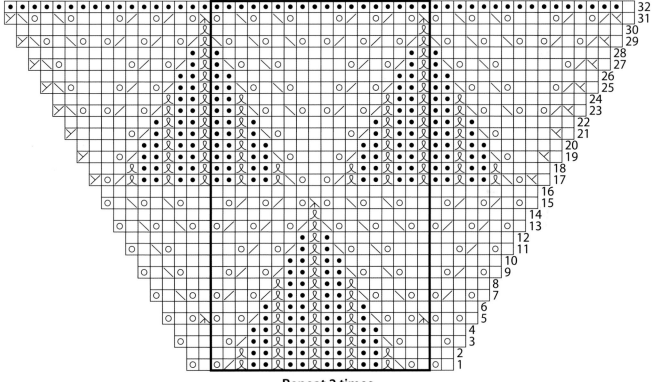

Repeat 2 times

— Repeat
☐ k
• p
Ꝉ k1 tbl
○ YO
⧄ M1R
⧅ M1L
╱ k2tog
╲ ssk
⋀ sl 1-k2tog-psso

Dash Panel

A simple lace motif takes on a bold modern appearance when worked in oversized yarn in Dash Panel. I find something comforting about working the same few rows over and over again and ending up with a whole that is somehow more than the sum of its parts. If you're wondering about the name, it comes from the video game *Mario Kart*. In the game there are strips with arrows on them embedded in the ground, and when you drive over them, they make your car go superfast! They're called Dash Panels—hence the name for this project.

Finished Size: 6 in. (15 cm) wide and 116 in. (294.5 cm) long

Yarn: Cascade Yarns Lana Grande (100% Peruvian highland wool; 87 yd./79.5 m; 3.5 oz./ 100 g); Pine Grove, 2 skeins, approximately 173 yds. (159 m)

Note: This pattern is designed to use as much of the yarn as possible. Depending on your gauge, you may end up with more or fewer repeats.

Needles: US size 15 (10 mm)

Notions: Tapestry needle

Gauge: 7 sts and 12 rows = 4 in. (10 cm) in St st, blocked; 8.5 sts and 10.5 rows = 4 in. (10 cm) in Lace Pattern, blocked

Special Stitches

CDD: Central double decrease; slip two stitches as if to k2tog, knit next stitch, and pass both slipped stitches over together. Two stitches decreased.

Stitch Guide

CHART WRITTEN INSTRUCTIONS

Row 1: K1, k2tog, YO, k1, YO, skp, k1, k2tog, YO, k1, YO, ssk, k1.

Rows 2 and 4: Sl 1 wyif, k1, purl to last 2 sts, k1, sl 1 wyif.

Row 3: K1, k2tog, YO, k2, YO, CDD, YO, k2, YO, ssk, k1.

Instructions

Using the Knitted Cast-On method (see page 111), CO 13 sts.

SET-UP
Rows 1 and 3 (RS): Knit.
Rows 2 and 4 (WS): Sl 1 wyif, knit to last st, sl 1 wyif.

BODY
Work Chart Rows 1–4 seventy-three times or until scarf is desired length. (See Stitch Guide above for written chart instructions.)

END
Rows 1 and 3 (RS): Knit.
Row 2 (WS): Sl 1 wyif, knit to last st, sl 1 wyif.

With WS facing and using the Expandable Lace Bind-Off, Knit Variant method (see page 112), BO all sts.

FINISHING
Weave in ends. Wet block to measurements. Trim ends.

Chart

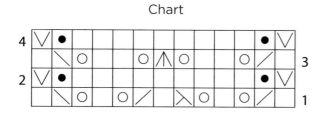

	RS: k; WS: p
•	WS: k
○	YO
╱	k2tog
╲	ssk
⤬	skp
⋀	CDD
⋁	WS: sl 1 wyif

Un, Deux, Trois

As I was knitting this shawl, the phrase "as simple as one, two, three" kept going through my mind; French just sounds fancier. To create this crescent shape, you will increase by six stitches every two rows—three stitches on each edge. By keeping all the lace repeats divisible by three, I created three sizes of diamonds that flow seamlessly into one another.

Finished Size: 20 in. (51 cm) deep and 61 in. (155 cm) wingspan

Yarn: Miss Babs K2 (100% merino wool; 240 yd./ 219 m; 7.2 oz./200 g); Dark Adobe, 2 skeins, approximately 451 yd. (412 m)

Note: This pattern uses up more than 90% of the yarn in 2 skeins; if you are not accurate to gauge, you should buy an extra skein.

Needles: US size 11 (8 mm) 47 in. (120 cm) circular needle

Notions: Tapestry needle

Gauge: 9.5 sts and 18 rows = 4 in. (10 cm) in St st, blocked; 8 sts and 16 rows = 4 in. (10 cm) in Lace Pattern, blocked

Special Stitches

kYOk: Knit, yarn over, knit; knit into the front loop of next stitch as usual but leave it on the needle, YO, then knit into the same stitch again. Two stitches increased.

sl 1-k2tog-psso: Slip one, knit two together, pass slipped stitch over; slip one stitch as to knit, knit the next two stitches together as one, insert left-hand needle into the front loop of the slipped stitch from left to right and pass it over the k2tog stitch and drop it off the needle. Two stitches decreased.

Stitch Guide

LACE PATTERN ONE

Row 1: K2, kYOk, *k3, YO, sl 1-k2tog-psso, YO; rep from * to last 6 sts, k3, kYOk, k2—4 sts inc'd.

Row 2: Sl 1 wyif, k1, YO, purl to last 2 sts, YO, k1, sl 1 wyif—2 sts inc'd.

Rep Rows 1 and 2 for pattern.

LACE PATTERN TWO

Row 1: K2, kYOk, k2, *YO, skp, k1, k2tog, YO, k1; rep from * to last 4 sts, k1, kYOk, k2—4 sts inc'd.

Row 2: Sl 1 wyif, k1, YO, purl to last 2 sts, YO, k1, sl 1 wyif—2 sts inc'd.

Row 3: K2, kYOk, *YO, sl 1-k2tog-psso, YO, k3; rep from * to last 6 sts, YO, sl 1-k2tog-psso, YO, kYOk, k2—4 sts inc'd.

Row 4: Sl 1 wyif, k1, YO, purl to last 2 sts, YO, k1, sl 1 wyif—2 sts inc'd.

Row 5: K2, kYOk, k2, *k2tog, YO, k1, YO, skp, k1; rep from * to last 4 sts, k1, kYOk, k2—4 sts inc'd.

Row 6: Sl 1 wyif, k1, YO, purl to last 2 sts, YO, k1, sl 1 wyif—2 sts inc'd.

CHART A WRITTEN INSTRUCTIONS

Row 1: K2, kYOk, [k3, (YO, skp) twice, k1, (k2tog, YO) twice] 16 times, k3, kYOk, k2—205 sts.

Row 2: Sl 1 wyif, k1, YO, purl to last 2 sts, YO, k1, sl 1 wyif—207 sts.

Row 3: K2, kYOk, k2tog, YO, k1, (k4, YO, skp, YO, sl 1-k2tog-psso, YO, k2tog, YO, k1) 16 times, k4, YO, skp, kYOk, k2—211 sts.

Row 4: Sl 1 wyif, k1, YO, purl to last 2 sts, YO, k1, sl 1 wyif—213 sts.

Row 5: K2, kYOk, k2, k2tog, YO, k2, (k5, YO, skp, k1, k2tog, YO, k2) 16 times, k5, YO, skp, k2, kYOk, k2—217 sts.

Row 6: Sl 1 wyif, k1, YO, purl to last 2 sts, YO, k1, sl 1 wyif—219 sts.

Row 7: K2, kYOk, k3, YO, sl 1-k2tog-psso, YO, k1, YO, skp, (k3, k2tog, YO, k1, YO, sl 1-k2tog-psso, YO, k1, YO, skp) 16 times, k3, k2tog, YO, k1, YO, sl 1-k2tog-psso, YO, k3, kYOk, k2—223 sts.

Row 8: Sl 1 wyif, k1, YO, purl to last 2 sts, YO, k1, sl 1 wyif—225 sts.

CHART B WRITTEN INSTRUCTIONS

Row 1: K2, kYOk, k1, [k1, (k2tog, YO) twice, k3, (YO, skp) twice] 18 times, k2, kYOk, k2—229 sts.

Row 2: Sl 1 wyif, k1, YO, purl to last 2 sts, YO, k1, sl 1 wyif—231 sts.

Row 3: K2, kYOk, k1, YO, skp, YO, (sl 1-k2tog-psso, YO, k2tog, YO, k1, YO, sl 1-k2tog-psso, YO, k1, YO, skp, YO) 18 times, sl 1-k2tog-psso, YO, k3, kYOk, k2—235 sts.

Instructions

Using the Cable Cast-On method (see page 109), CO 9 sts.

SET-UP

Row 1 (RS): K2, kYOk, k3, kYOk, k2—13 sts.

Row 2 (WS): Sl 1 wyif, k1, YO, k9, YO, k1, sl 1 wyif—15 sts.

BODY

*Work Lace Pattern One 6 times—51 sts. (See Stitch Guide at left for written instructions.)

Work Lace Pattern Two once—69 sts. (See Stitch Guide at left for written instructions.)

Rep from * twice, then work Lace Pattern One 4 more times—201 sts.

Work Chart A Rows 1–8 once. (See Stitch Guide at left for written chart instructions.)

Work Chart B Rows 1–3 once. (See Stitch Guide at left for written chart instructions.)

Chart A

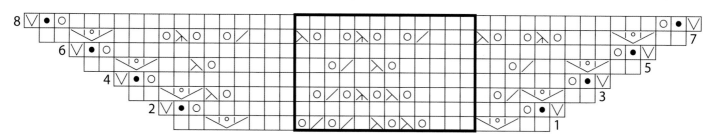

Repeat 16 times

Chart B

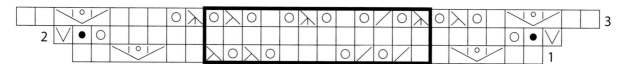

Repeat 18 times

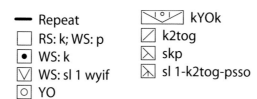

── Repeat	⊻⊡⊻	kYOk
▢ RS: k; WS: p	⧄	k2tog
⊡ WS: k	⧅	skp
⋁ WS: sl 1 wyif	⧆	sl 1-k2tog-psso
⊙ YO		

FINISHING

With the WS facing and using the Expandable Lace Bind-Off, Knit Variant method (see page 112), BO all sts.

Wet block to final measurements. Trim ends.

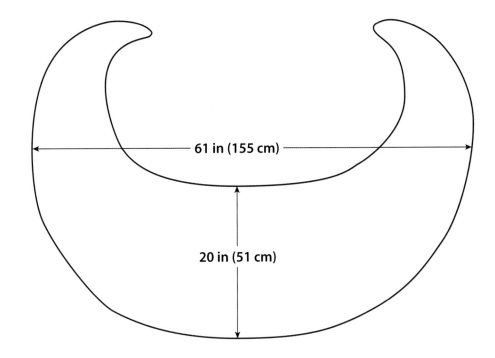

61 in (155 cm)

20 in (51 cm)

Bonus Stitch Hat

This hat features an element that can be slightly mystifying to novice lace knitters: a varying stitch count. Typically increases and decreases are paired in the same row to maintain your stitch count. But the forgiving nature of lace allows you to put off fixing an unbalanced pairing until later. In the Bonus Stitch Hat, you'll feel like you have a bonus stitch, but don't worry—Round 5 has a special stitch that brings everything back into balance.

Finished Size: 18.5 in. (47 cm) brim circumference and 9.25 in. (23.5 cm) tall

Yarn: MollyGirl Rock Star XL (100% merino wool; 100 yd./91 m; 5.3 oz./150 g); Riptide, 1 skein, approximately 70 yd. (64 m)

Needles: US size 10 (6 mm) 16 in. (40.5 cm) circular needle and set of dpns or your choice of small-circumference knitting needles (see Knitting in the Round, page 108)

Notions: Stitch marker, tapestry needle

Gauge: 12 sts and 18 rows = 4 in. (10 cm) in St st in the rnd, blocked

Special Stitches

sl 1-k2tog-psso: Slip one, knit two together, pass slipped stitch over; slip one stitch as to knit, knit the next two stitches together as one, insert left-hand needle into the front loop of the slipped stitch from left to right and pass it over the k2tog stitch and drop it off the needle. Two stitches decreased.

sl 1-k2-psso: Slip one, knit two, pass slipped stitch over; slip one stitch as to knit, knit the next two stitches, insert left-hand needle into the front loop of the slipped stitch from left to right and pass it over the two knit stitches and drop it off the needle. One stitch decreased.

Stitch Guide

BODY CHART WRITTEN INSTRUCTIONS

Note: The st count increases to 64 sts on Rnd 1 and returns to 56 on Rnd 5.

Rnd 1: (K4, YO, k3) 8 times—64 sts.
Rnds 2, 4, and 6: Knit.
Rnd 3: (K2, k2tog, YO, k1, YO, ssk, k1) 8 times.
Rnd 5: (K1, k2tog, YO, sl 1-k2-psso, YO, ssk) 8 times—56 sts.

Rep Rnds 1–6 for pattern.

CROWN CHART WRITTEN INSTRUCTIONS
Rnd 1: (K3, ssk, k6, YO, k3) 4 times—56 sts.
Rnds 2, 4, 6, 10, 12, and 14: Knit.
Rnd 3: (K1, ssk, k1, k2tog, k2, k2tog, YO, k1, YO, ssk, k1) 4 times—48 sts.

Rnd 5: (K1, sl 1-k2tog-psso, k1, k2tog, YO, sl 1-k2-psso, YO, ssk) 4 times—36 sts.
Rnd 7: Remove EOR m, sl 1 pwise to RH needle, replace EOR m for new EOR, (k1, k2tog, YO, k1, ssk, k1, YO, ssk) 4 times—32 sts.
Rnd 8: Knit to last st, sl st, remove EOR m, sl st pwise back to LH needle, replace m for new EOR.
Rnd 9: (Sl 1-k2tog-psso, k1, YO, sl 1-k2tog-psso, YO, k1) 4 times—24 sts.
Rnd 11: (K1, k2tog, k1, ssk) 4 times—16 sts.
Rnd 13: (K1, sl 1-k2tog-psso) 4 times—8 sts.

Instructions

Using the Cable Cast-On method (see page 109), CO 56 sts. Pm to indicate EOR and join to work in the rnd, being careful not to twist sts.

BRIM

Rnd 1: *K1, p1; rep from * to EOR.
Rep Rnd 1 three more times.

BODY

Work Body Chart 5 times, working chart 8 times around each rnd. (See Stitch Guide at left for written chart instructions.)

Work Crown Chart once, working chart 4 times around each rnd, switching to dpns or your preferred small-circumference knitting method when the number of sts gets too small for the 16 in. (40.5 cm) needle. (See Stitch Guide at left for written chart instructions.)

FINISHING

Break yarn leaving a 7 in. (18 cm) tail.

Thread tail onto tapestry needle and pull through remaining sts. Pull tail to cinch closed.

Weave in ends. Wet block over bowl or balloon, being careful to not stretch the ribbing. Trim ends.

Body Chart

Repeat 8 times

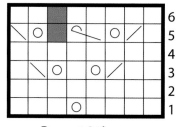

— Repeat
▨ No stitch
☐ k
◉ YO
╱ k2tog
╲ ssk
⋌ sl 1-k2tog-psso
⋋ sl 1-k2-psso
★ First st of round only: remove EOR m, sl st pwise to RH needle, replace EOR m, new EOR.
✦ k; on last rep no stitch: sl st, remove EOR m, sl st pwise back to LH needle, replace EOR m, new EOR.

Crown Chart

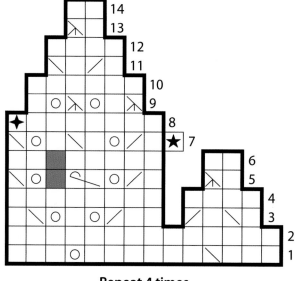

Repeat 4 times

Drunk Spider

Despite initial appearances, the lace pattern in this warm weather accessory is actually quite regular. It's the thick and thin nature of the soft cotton yarn that creates a somewhat wonky effect. While knitting lace, I am often reminded of spiders spinning webs, but it amuses me to think that perhaps the spider spinning the web for this project may have overindulged. Once Drunk Spider is blocked, the effect isn't so pronounced, but as you are knitting, see whether things don't appear a bit tipsy!

Finished Size: 27 in. (68.5 cm) neck circumference, 14.5 in. (37 cm) long in front, and 9.25 in. (23.5 cm) long in back

Yarn: Knit Picks Billow (100% cotton; 120 yd./110 m; 3.53 oz./100 g); Turmeric, 1 skein, approximately 105 yd. (96 m)

Needles: US size 11 (8 mm) 24 in. (60 cm) circular needle (see Knitting in the Round, page 108)

Notions: 2 stitch markers, tapestry needle

Gauge: 11 sts and 14 rows = 4 in. (10 cm) in St st in the rnd, blocked; 11.5 sts and 16 rows = 4 in. (10 cm) in Lace Pattern in the rnd, blocked

sl m, k1, YO, *k1, k2tog, YO twice, ssk, k3; rep from * to EOR—2 sts inc'd.

Rnd 8: *K3, p1, k4; rep from * to 7 sts before m, k3, p1, k3, sl m, k2, *k3, p1, k4; rep from * to 8 sts before EOR, k3, p1, k3, sl st, remove EOR m, sl st pwise back to LH needle, replace EOR m for new EOR.

CHART B WRITTEN INSTRUCTIONS

Rnd 1: *Ssk, k4, k2tog, YO twice; rep from * to m, sl m, k1, YO twice, *ssk, k4, k2tog, YO twice; rep from * to EOR—2 sts inc'd.

Rnd 2: *K7, p1; rep from * to m, sl m, k1, p1, k1, *k7, p1; rep from * to EOR.

Rnd 3: *YO, ssk, k2, k2tog, YO, k2; rep from * to m, YO, sl m, k1, YO, k2, *YO, ssk, k2, k2tog, YO, k2; rep from * to EOR—2 sts inc'd.

Rnds 4 and 6: Knit.

Rnd 5: *K1, YO, ssk, k2tog, YO, k3; rep from * to 1 st before m, k1, YO, sl m, k1, YO, k3, *k1, YO, ssk, k2tog, YO, k3; rep from * to EOR—2 sts inc'd.

Rnd 7: *K1, k2tog, YO twice, ssk, k3; rep from * to 2 st before m, k2, YO, sl m, k1, YO, k4, *k1, k2tog, YO twice, ssk, k3; rep from * to EOR—2 sts inc'd.

Rnd 8: *K3, p1, k4; rep from * to 3 sts before m, k3, sl m, k6, *k3, p1, k4; rep from * to 8 sts before EOR, k3, p1, k3, sl st, remove EOR m, sl st pwise back to LH needle, replace EOR m for new EOR.

Instructions

Using the Knitted Cast-On method (see page 111), CO 55 sts. Pm to indicate EOR and join to work in the rnd, being careful not to twist sts.

SET-UP

Rnd 1: (P1, k1) 13 times, YO, pm, k1, YO, (p1, k1) 14 times—57 sts.

Rnd 2: *K1, p1; rep from * to 1 st before m, k1, sl m, k2, *k1, p1; rep from * to EOR.

SECTION A

Work Chart A Rnds 1–8. (See Stitch Guide at left for written chart instructions.)

Stitch Guide

CHART A WRITTEN INSTRUCTIONS

Rnd 1: *Ssk, k4, k2tog, YO twice; rep from * to 4 sts before m, ssk, k2, YO, sl m, k1, YO, k2, k2tog, YO twice, *ssk, k4, k2tog, YO twice; rep from * to EOR—2 sts inc'd.

Rnd 2: *K7, p1; rep from * to 4 sts before m, k4, sl m, k6, p1, *k7, p1; rep from * to EOR.

Rnd 3: *YO, ssk, k2, k2tog, YO, k2; rep from * to 4 sts before m, YO, ssk, k2, YO, sl m, k1, YO, k2, k2tog, YO, k2, *YO, ssk, k2, k2tog, YO, k2; rep from * to EOR—2 sts inc'd.

Rnd 4: Knit.

Rnd 5: *K1, YO, ssk, k2tog, YO, k3; rep from * to 5 sts before m, k1, YO, ssk, k2tog, YO twice, sl m, k1, YO twice, ssk, k2tog, YO, k3, *k1, YO, ssk, k2tog, YO, k3; rep from * to EOR—2 sts inc'd.

Rnd 6: Knit to 2 sts before m, p1, k1, sl m, k2, p1, knit to EOR.

Rnd 7: *K1, k2tog, YO twice, ssk, k3; rep from * to 6 sts before m, k1, k2tog, YO twice, ssk, k1, YO,

Note: Don't knit the last st of the last rep of Rnd 8, sl st, remove EOR m, sl st pwise back to LH needle, replace EOR m for new EOR—65 sts.

SECTION B

Work Chart B Rnds 1–8. (See Stitch Guide at left for written chart instructions.)

Note: Don't knit the last st of the last rep of Rnd 8, sl st, remove EOR m, sl st pwise back to LH needle, replace EOR m for new EOR—73 sts.

Rep Charts A and B once more; then work Chart A Rnd 1 once more—91 sts.

END

Using the Expandable Lace Bind-Off, Knit Variant method (see page 112), BO all sts with the following modification: when working into a double YO, allow one of the loops to fall off the needle and BO into the resulting oversized st 4 times.

FINISHING

Break yarn leaving a 7 in. (18 cm) tail. Using the long tail threaded onto a tapestry needle, neaten the join at the EOR. Weave in ends.

Wet block to finished measurements. Steam out any crease lines where piece was blocked flat. Trim ends.

▨	No stitch
☐	k
⊡	p
⊙	YO
⧄	k2tog
⧅	ssk
✦	k; on last rep no stitch: sl st, remove EOR m, sl st pwise back to LH needle, replace EOR m, new EOR.
▬	Repeat
▬	Stitch Marker

Chart A

Stitch Marker

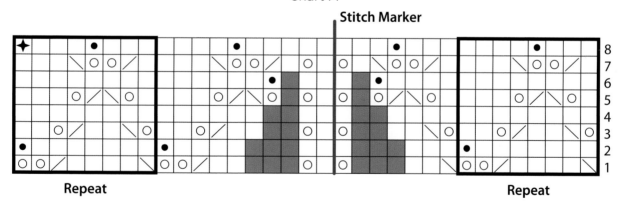

Repeat **Repeat**

Chart B

Stitch Marker

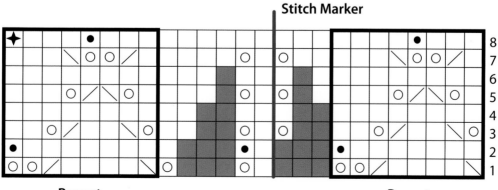

Repeat **Repeat**

Shorty Squiggle Mitts

Most of the time the way I describe blocking lace varies between "aggressive" and "assertive." But for the Shorty Squiggle Mitts, the word "gently" is essential. The marriage of the lace stitch and the yarn combines into a wonderful texture that I hate to lose. If you are unsure about what size to make, consider erring on the larger size so that your hand doesn't stretch it out too much.

Sizes: S/M (L/XL)

Finished Size: 7 (8.75) in. [17.75 (22.25) cm] around and 7 in. (17.75 cm) long

Yarn: Berroco Vintage Chunky (50% acrylic, 40% wool, 10% nylon; 136 yd./124 m; 3.53 oz./100 g); Oatmeal, 1 skein, approximately 66 yd. (61 m)

Needles: *Ribbing:* US size 10 (6 mm) set of dpns or your choice of small-circumference knitting needles; *Body:* US size 10.5 (6.5 mm) set of dpns or your choice of small-circumference knitting needles (see Knitting in the Round, page 108)

Notions: Stitch marker, tapestry needle

Gauge: 13 sts and 20 rows = 4 in. (10 cm) in St st in the rnd, on larger needle, blocked; 13.5 sts and 19.5 rows = 4 in. (10 cm) in Squiggle Pattern in the rnd, blocked

Special Stitches

M1PR: Make one purl right; using the left needle, pick up the strand of yarn that runs between the last stitch worked and the next stitch to be worked from back to front, and purl this strand through the front loop. One stitch increased.

sl 1-k2tog-psso: Slip one, knit two together, pass slipped stitch over; slip one stitch as to knit, knit the next two stitches together as one, insert left-hand needle into the front loop of the slipped stitch from left to right and pass it over the k2tog stitch and drop it off the needle. Two stitches decreased.

Stitch Guide

PURL RIBBING
Rnd 1: *P1, k1; rep from * to EOR.
Rep Rnd 1 for pattern.

KNIT RIBBING
Rnd 1: *K1, p1; rep from * to EOR.
Rep Rnd 1 for pattern.

CHART WRITTEN INSTRUCTIONS
Rnd 1: *P1, k5; rep from * to EOR.
Rnd 2: Rep Rnd 1.
Rnd 3: *K1, YO, skp, p1, k2tog, YO; rep from * to EOR.
Rnd 4: *K3, p1, k2; rep from * to EOR.
Rnds 5 and 6: Rep Rnd 4.
Rnd 7: *P1, k2tog, YO, k1, YO, skp; rep from * to EOR.
Rnd 8: Rep Rnd 1.

Rep Rnds 1–8 for pattern.

Instructions

Using smaller needle and the Long Tail Cast-On method (see page 111), CO 24 (30) sts. Pm to indicate EOR and join to work in the rnd, being careful not to twist sts.

Work Purl Ribbing for 5 rnds. Switch to larger needle.

Work Chart Rnds 1–6, working chart 4 (5) times around each rnd. (See Stitch Guide at left for written chart instructions.)

THUMB GUSSET
Rnd 1: M1PR, YO, pm, work chart 4 (5) times around—26 (32) sts.
Rnd 2: P1, knit to m, sl m, work chart 4 (5) times around.
Rnd 3: P1, YO, knit to m, YO, sl m, work chart 4 (5) times around—28 (34) sts.
Rnd 4: P1, knit to m, sl m, work chart 4 (5) times around.

Modify Me!
I designed these mitts to be short, but if you want them to be arm warmers, simply repeat Rounds 1–8 of the stitch pattern a time or two between the ribbing and the beginning of the thumb gusset (but make sure to start the gusset after Round 6).

Rnd 5: K1, YO, knit to m, YO, sl m, work chart 4 (5) times around—30 (36) sts.

Rnd 6: Knit to m, sl m, work chart 4 (5) times around.

Rnds 7 and 8: Rep Rnds 5 and 6—32 (38) sts.

Rnds 9 and 10: Rep Rnds 3 and 4—34 (40) sts.

Transfer 10 Thumb Gusset sts to waste yarn, rm—24 (30) sts.

HAND

Work Chart Rnds 1–7, working chart 4 (5) times around each rnd.

Next Rnd: (P1, k5) 3 (4) times, p1, k4, sl 1, remove EOR m, sl st back to LH needle, replace m for new EOR.

Next Rnd: *Sl 1-k2tog-psso, YO, k3, YO; rep from * to EOR.

Switch to smaller needle.

Work Knit Ribbing for 4 rnds.

Using the 1x1 Ribbing Bind-Off method (see page 112), BO all sts.

THUMB

Remount 10 Thumb Gusset sts to larger needle. Pick up and knit 2 sts where the thumb meets the hand, pm to indicate EOR—12 sts.

Knit 3 rnds. Switch to smaller needle.

Work 2 rnds of Purl Ribbing. Using the 1x1 Ribbing Bind-Off method (see page 112), BO all sts.

FINISHING

Weave in ends, using tails to neaten joins where the thumb meets the hand. Wet block gently to final measurements. Trim ends.

Repeat for second mitt.

Chart

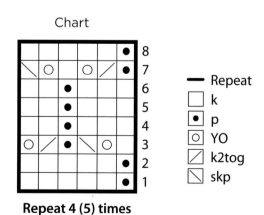

Repeat 4 (5) times

— Repeat
☐ k
⊡ p
⊙ YO
╱ k2tog
╲ skp

Hearts in Chains Poncho

Are you looking for a wrap with a good bit of lace that will still keep you warm? This is the accessory for you! The body of this snuggly poncho is worked in stockinette and provides plenty of insulation. The lace along the bottom edge gives you lovely openwork without compromising cold-weather comfort.

Finished Size: 26 in. (66 cm) wide and 52 in. (132 cm) long, before seaming

Yarn: Cascade Yarns Eco+ (100% Peruvian highland wool; 478 yd./437 m; 8.75 oz./250 g); Irelande, 2 skeins, approximately 780 yd. (713 m)

Needles: US size 10 (6 mm) 47 in. (120 cm) circular needle

Notions: Tapestry needle, 2 stitch markers

Gauge: 13.5 sts and 22 rows = 4 in. (10 cm) in St st, blocked

Special Stitches

sl 1-k2tog-psso: Slip one, knit two together, pass slipped stitch over; slip one stitch as to knit, knit the next two stitches together as one, insert left-hand needle into the front loop of the slipped stitch from left to right and pass it over the k2tog stitch and drop it off the needle. Two stitches decreased.

ssk-pssf-sl 1: Slip, slip, knit, pass slipped stitch forward, slip; ssk, then return new stitch to left-hand needle, pass the second stitch on left-hand needle over the ssk stitch and off the needle, slip ssk stitch purlwise back to right-hand needle. Two stitches decreased.

Stitch Guide

CHART WRITTEN INSTRUCTIONS

Row 1: (K2tog, YO) twice, k5, (YO, ssk) twice, k3, (k2tog, YO) twice, k5, (YO, ssk) twice, k1.

Row 2 (and all WS rows): Purl.

Row 3: K2, (YO, ssk) twice, k1, (k2tog, YO) twice, k4, (k2tog, YO) twice, k1, YO, ssk, k1, (k2tog, YO) twice, k3.

Row 5: K3, YO, ssk, YO, sl 1-k2tog-psso, YO, k2tog, YO, k4, (k2tog, YO) twice, k1, YO, ssk, YO, ssk-pssf-sl 1, YO, k2tog, YO, k4.

Row 7: K5, (k2tog, YO) twice, k4, (k2tog, YO) twice, k3, (YO, ssk) twice, k6.

Row 9: K4, k2tog, YO, k1, (YO, ssk) twice, k1, (k2tog, YO) twice, k5, (YO, ssk) twice, k5.

Row 11: K3, (k2tog, YO) twice, k1, YO, ssk, YO, sl 1-k2tog-psso, YO, k2tog, YO, k4, (k2tog, YO) twice, k1, (YO, ssk) twice, k2.

Row 13: K2, (k2tog, YO) twice, k3, YO, ssk, YO, sl 1-k2tog-psso, YO, k4, (k2tog, YO) twice, k3, (YO, ssk) twice, k1.

Row 15: K1, (k2tog, YO) twice, k5, (YO, ssk) twice, k3, (k2tog, YO) twice, k5, (YO, ssk) twice.

Row 17: K3, (YO, ssk) twice, k1, k2tog, YO, k1, (YO, ssk) twice, k4, (YO, ssk) twice, k1, (k2tog, YO) twice, k2.

Row 19: K4, YO, ssk, YO, sl 1-k2tog-psso, YO, k2tog, YO, k1, (YO, ssk) twice, k4, YO, ssk, YO, ssk-pssf-sl 1, YO, k2tog, YO, k3.

Row 21: K6, (k2tog, YO) twice, k3, (YO, ssk) twice, k4, (YO, ssk) twice, k5.

Row 23: K5, (k2tog, YO) twice, k5, (YO, ssk) twice, k1, (k2tog, YO) twice, k1, YO, ssk, k4.

Row 25: K2, (k2tog, YO) twice, k1, (YO, ssk) twice, k4, YO, ssk, YO, ssk-pssf-sl 1, YO, k2tog, YO, k1, (YO, ssk) twice, k3.

Row 27: K1, (k2tog, YO) twice, k3, (YO, ssk) twice, k4, YO, ssk-pssf-sl 1, YO, k2tog, YO, k3, (YO ssk) twice, k2.

Instructions

Using the Cable Cast-On method (see page 109), CO 89 sts.

SET-UP

Row 1 (RS): *K1, p1; rep from * to last st, sl 1 wyif.

Row 2 (WS): K1, *k1, p1; rep from * to last 2 sts, k1, sl 1 wyif.

Rep Rows 1 and 2 once more.

BODY

Row 1: K55, pm, work Row 1 of chart, pm, k3, sl 1 wyif. (See Stitch Guide above for written instructions.)

Row 2 (and all WS rows): K2, purl to last 2 sts, k1, sl 1 wyif.

Work as established on RS and WS rows, slipping m and continuing chart until you have completed 9 full reps. Then work Chart Rows 1–14 once more.

END
Row 1 (RS): *K1, p1; rep from * to last st, sl 1 wyif.
Row 2 (WS): K1, *k1, p1; rep from * to last 2 sts, k1, sl 1 wyif.

Rep Rows 1 and 2 once more.

Using the 1x1 Ribbing Bind-Off method (see page 112), BO all sts.

FINISHING
Weave in ends. Wet block to size. Trim ends.

Fold piece with WS together, CO and BO edges aligned, and lace panel at the bottom. Along the top edge, mark 14 in. (35.5 cm) from the fold and seam from that point toward the open edge using your preferred method. Steam the seam to neaten if desired. Weave in and trim ends.

Modify Me!
By reducing the number of stitches in the stockinette section of this pattern, you can create a poncho that isn't as long on your torso. So if you are looking for something shorter, take out some stitches.

Chart

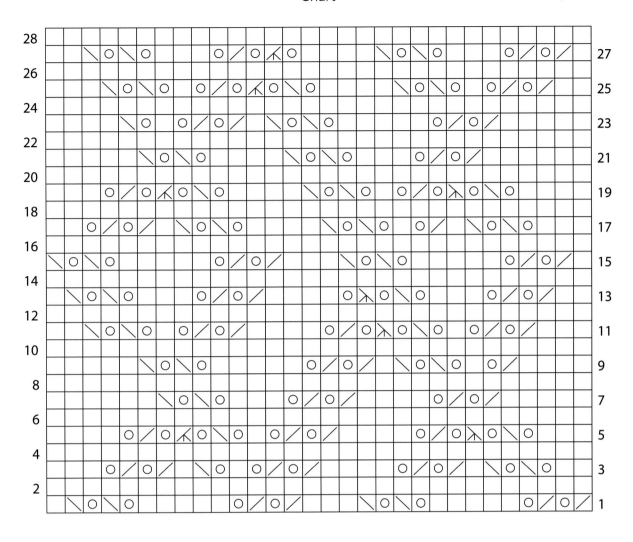

☐ RS: k; WS: p
◎ YO
⊘ k2tog
◪ ssk
⧄ sl 1-k2tog-psso
⧅ ssk-pssf-sl 1

Rupee Slouch

In the Kingdom of Hyrule, the unit of currency is the rupee. Even if you are not familiar with the *Legend of Zelda* games, you can guess what shape a rupee is just by looking at this hat. But you don't have to be a gamer to wear this fun, slouchy accessory.

Finished Size: 18.5 in. (47 cm) around and 10.75 in. (27.5 cm) tall

Yarn: Anzula Burly (80% merino, 10% cashmere, 10% nylon; 100 yd./91 m; 4.02 oz./114 g); Paprika, 1 skein, approximately 65 yd. (59.5 m)

Needles: *Brim:* US size 13 (9 mm) 16 in. (40.5 cm) circular needle; *Body:* US size 15 (10 mm) 16 in. (40.5 cm) circular needle and set of dpns or your choice of small-circumference knitting needles (see Knitting in the Round, page 108)

Notions: Stitch marker, tapestry needle

Gauge: 10 sts and 14 rows = 4 in. (10 cm) in St st in the rnd on larger needle, blocked; 10 sts and 15 rows = 4 in. (10 cm) in Lace Pattern in the rnd on larger needle, blocked

Special Stitches

sl 1-k2tog-psso: Slip one, knit two together, pass slipped stitch over; slip one stitch as to knit, knit the next two stitches together as one, insert left-hand needle into the front loop of the slipped stitch from left to right and pass it over the k2tog stitch and drop it off the needle. Two stitches decreased.

Stitch Guide

BODY CHART WRITTEN INSTRUCTIONS

Rnds 1, 3, and 5: (K1, YO, ssk, k2tog, YO) 10 times.

Rnd 2 and all even rnds: Knit.

Rnd 7: (K1, YO, ssk, k5, k2tog, YO) 5 times.

Rnd 9: (K2, YO, ssk, k3, k2tog, YO, k1) 5 times.

Rnd 11: (K3, YO, ssk, k1, k2tog, YO, k2) 5 times.

Rnd 13: (K4, YO, sl 1-k2tog-psso, YO, k3) 5 times.

Rnds 15, 17, and 19: (K1, YO, ssk, k2tog, YO) 10 times.

Rnd 21: (K3, k2tog, YO, k1, YO, ssk, k2) 5 times.

CROWN CHART WRITTEN INSTRUCTIONS

Rnd 1: (K2, k2tog, YO, k3, YO, ssk, k1) 5 times.

Rnd 2: (K4, sl 1-k2tog-psso, k3) 5 times—40 sts.

Rnd 3: (K1, k2tog, YO, k3, YO, ssk) 5 times.

Rnd 4: (K3, sl 1-k2tog-psso, k2) 5 times—30 sts.

Note: Don't knit the last st of the last rep of Rnd 4, sl st, remove EOR m, sl st pwise back to LH needle, replace EOR m for new EOR.

Rnd 5: (Sl 1-k2tog-psso, YO, k3, YO) 5 times.

Rnd 6: (K2, sl 1-k2tog-psso, k1) 5 times—20 sts.

Rnd 7: Knit.

Rnd 8: (K1, sl 1-k2tog-psso) 5 times—10 sts.

Instructions

Using smaller needle and the Long Tail Cast-On method (see page 111), CO 50 sts. Pm to indicate EOR and join to work in the rnd, being careful not to twist sts.

Modify Me!

This hat can be easily converted into a cowl by adding ten stitches—one repeat—to the cast-on and by replacing the crown decrease with ribbing just as you worked for the brim.

BRIM

Ribbing Rnd: P1, k1, *p2, k1, p1, k1; rep from * to last 3 sts, p2, k1.

Rep Ribbing Rnd 7 more times.

BODY

Switch to larger needle.

Work Body Chart Rnds 1–22 once, working chart 5 times around each rnd. (See Stitch Guide on page 84 for written chart instructions.)

Work Crown Chart Rnds 1–8 once, working chart 4 times around each rnd—10 sts. (See Stitch Guide on page 84 for written chart instructions.)

Next Rnd: (K1, ssk) 3 times, k1—7 sts.

FINISHING

Break yarn leaving a 7 in. (18 cm) tail. Thread tail onto tapestry needle and pull through remaining sts. Pull tail to cinch closed.

Weave in ends. Wet block over bowl or balloon, being careful to not stretch the ribbing. Trim ends.

Body Chart

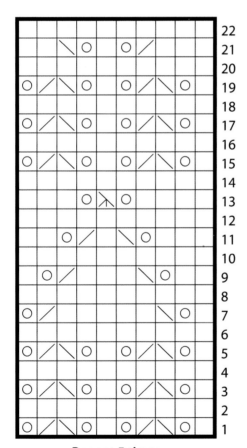

Repeat 5 times

— Repeat
�- No stitch
☐ k
⊙ YO
╱ k2tog
╲ ssk
⋉ sl 1-k2tog-psso
✦ k; on last rep no stitch:
sl st, remove EOR m,
sl st pwise back to LH
needle, replace EOR m,
new EOR.

Crown Chart

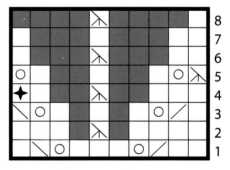

Repeat 5 times

Avasarala

Somewhere between a cowl and a poncho, Avasarala can be worn in numerous creative ways. It starts as a single piece before dividing into legs that are each half the width of the original cast-on. The legs are then reunited and grafted together, forming the loop of the cowl. The circumference is generous; you can wrap it around twice and still have plenty left over to tuck into a jacket to keep you toasty warm.

Finished Size: 75 in. (109.5 cm) circumference and 17.5 in. (44.5 cm) wide, 50 in. (127 cm) total length

Yarn: Malabrigo Chunky (100% merino; 100 yd./ 91 m; 3.5 oz./100 g); Stone Blue, 3 skeins, approximately 266 yd. (243 m)

Needles: US size 11 (8 mm)

Notions: 2 stitch markers, waste yarn

Gauge: 4 in. (10 cm) = 11 sts and 14 rows in Seed Stitch, blocked

Note

- Due to the size and complexity of the charts, this pattern does not include written instructions for the lace.

Instructions

Using the Long Tail Cast-On method (see page 111), CO 49 sts.

Set-Up Row (WS): Knit to last st, sl 1 wyif.
Row 1 (RS): Knit to last st, sl 1 wyif.
Row 2 (WS): K5, (p1, k1) 3 times, pm, p1, *k1, p1; rep from * to m, pm, (k1, p1) 3 times, k4, sl 1 wyif.

BODY

Row 1: Work Right Chart Row 1, sl m, (p1, k1) 13 times, p1, sl m, work Left Chart Row 1.

Row 2: Work Left Chart Row 2, sl m, p1, *k1, p1; rep from * to m, sl m, work Right Chart Row 2.
Row 3: Work Right Chart Row 3, sl m, *p1, k1; rep from * to 1 st before m, p1, sl m, work Left Chart Row 3.

Continue in patterns as established, ending with Row 30 of both charts.

Transition 1

Rows 1–3: Knit to last st, sl 1 wyif.
Row 4: K5, (p1, k1) 3 times, sl m, p1, *k1, p1; rep from * to m, sl m, (k1, p1) 3 times, k4, sl 1 wyif.

Left Chart

	RS: k; WS: p
●	RS: p; WS: k
⋁	WS: sl 1 wyif
⋈	sl 1 wyif
○	YO
╱	k2tog

Right Chart

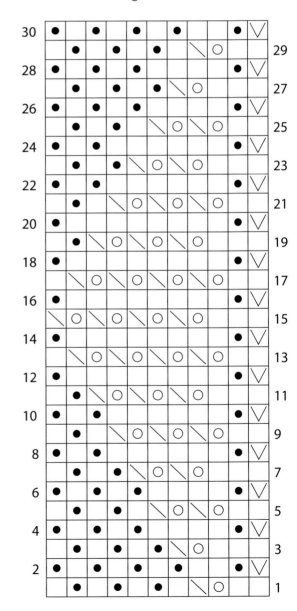

DIVIDE FOR RIGHT AND LEFT LEGS

Right Leg (worked over 24 sts)

Row 1 (RS): Work Right Chart Row 1, sl m, (p1, k1) 6 times, sl 1 wyif.

Transfer remaining stitches and m to waste yarn for *Left Leg*.

Row 2 (WS): K1, *k1, p1; rep from * to m, work Right Chart Row 2.

Continue in pattern as established, ending with Row 30 of Right Chart.

Transition 2

Rows 1–3: Knit to last st, sl 1 wyif.
Row 4: K1, *k1, p1; rep from * to m, sl m, (k1, p1) 3 times, k4, sl 1 wyif.

Work *Right Leg* (without transferring sts) followed by *Transition 2* twice more for a total of 3 complete reps of *Right Leg* and *Transition 2*.

Work *Right Leg* for Rows 1–16 of Right Chart as established.

Next Row (RS): Knit to last st, sl 1 wyif.

Cut yarn leaving a 7 in. (18 cm) tail to weave in. Transfer live sts to waste yarn and rm.

Left Leg (worked over 24 sts)

Remount held *Left Leg* sts onto needle. BO 1 st.

Note: The st on your RH needle resulting from the BO is the k1 in the first repeat of Row 1—24 sts.

Row 1 (RS): K1, *k1, p1; rep from * to m, sl m, Work Left Chart Row 1.
Row 2 (WS): Work Left Chart Row 2, sl m, *p1, k1; rep from * to last st, sl 1 wyif.

Continue in pattern as established, ending with Row 30 of Left Chart.

Transition 3

Rows 1–3: Knit to last st, sl 1 wyif.

Row 4: K5, (p1, k1) 3 times, sl m, p1, *k1, p1; rep from * to last st, sl 1 wyif.

Work *Left Leg* (without remounting or binding off a stitch) followed by *Transition 3* twice more for a total of 3 complete reps of *Left Leg* and *Transition 3*.

Work *Left Leg* for Rows 1–16 of Left Chart as established.

Next Row (RS): Knit to last st, sl 1 wyif.

Cut yarn leaving a 7 in. (18 cm) tail to weave in. Transfer live sts to waste yarn and rm.

FINISHING

Weave in ends. Wet block to a rectangle 17.5 x 50 in. (44.5 x 127 cm).

Transfer live sts onto 2 separate needles with WS facing and points to the right. The lace will be on the left and the solid sections on the right. Be sure not to twist. With a piece of yarn approximately 50 in. (127 cm) long, graft the sides using the Kitchener Stitch method (see page 113). Weave in remaining ends, using them to neaten the joins if needed. Trim ends.

Bitis Shawl

Bitis is the genus for a species of vipers that are known for inflating and deflating their bodies while loudly hissing. When I was blocking this shawl, I noticed that the stitch pattern flows in a sinuous motion down the shawl and ends with a shape evocative of a snake's head. I ended up Googling and finding a lot of cool snakes while trying to figure out a name for this fantastically bulky shawl that features generous use of double yarn overs.

Finished Size: 16 in. (40.5 cm) height, 55 in. (140 cm) wingspan, 75 in. (190.5 cm) along neckline

Yarn: Malabrigo Rasta (100% merino wool; 90 yd./82 m; 5.3 oz./150 g); Melon, 4 skeins, approximately 344 yd. (314.5 m)

Note: This pattern uses up more than 90% of the yarn in 4 skeins; if you are not accurate to gauge, you should buy an extra skein.

Needles: US size 17 (12 mm) 47 in. (120 cm) circular needle

Notions: Tapestry needle

Gauge: 7 sts and 10 rows = 4 in. (10 cm) in St st, blocked; 8 sts and 9 rows = 4 in. (10 cm) in Lace Pattern, blocked

Note

• Due to the size and complexity of the charts, this pattern does not include written instructions for the lace.

Instructions

Using the Cable Cast-On method (see page 109), CO 59 sts.

SET-UP
Row 1 (RS): K2, YO, k55, YO, k1, sl 1 wyif—61 sts.

Row 2 (WS): K2, k1fb, k55, k1fb, k1, sl 1 wyif— 63 sts.

Row 3: K2, *YO, k1; rep from * to last 2 sts, YO, k1, sl 1 wyif—123 sts.

Row 4: K2, k1fb, k2tog, k115, k1fb, k1, sl 1 wyif— 124 sts.

BODY
Work Chart A—148 sts.

Work Chart B—172 sts.

Work Chart C—194 sts.

Chart A

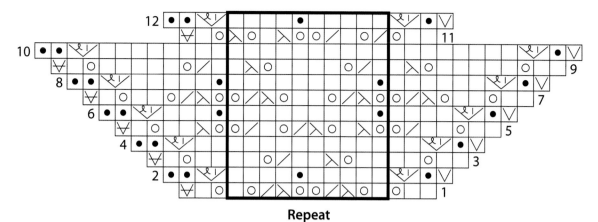

Repeat

Chart B

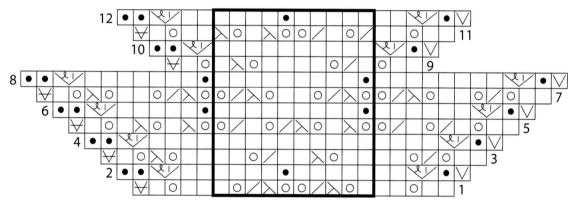

Repeat

Chart C

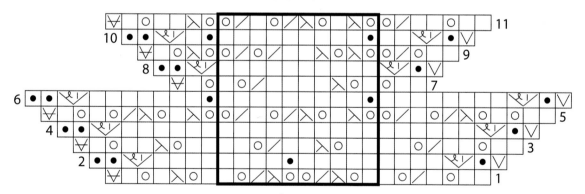

Repeat

— Repeat

☐ RS: k; WS: p

• WS: k

∨ WS: sl 1 wyif

⩔ sl 1 wyif

○ YO

⩔ WS: k1fb

╱ k2tog

⧄ skp

With WS facing, bind off as follows: K1, (k1, insert LH needle through the front loops of the 2 sts on the RH needle and k2tog tbl) 10 times, *insert LH needle through the front leg of the st on the RH needle and k1 tbl, p2tog, insert LH needle through the front loops of the 2 sts on the RH needle and k2tog tbl, insert LH needle through the front leg of the st on the RH needle and k1 tbl, (k1, insert LH needle through the front legs of the 2 sts on the RH needle and k2tog tbl) 8 times; rep from * to last 3 sts, (k1, insert LH needle through the front legs of the 2 sts on the RH needle and k2tog tbl) 3 times.

FINISHING

Weave in ends. Wet block, curving the top edge (see schematic). Trim ends.

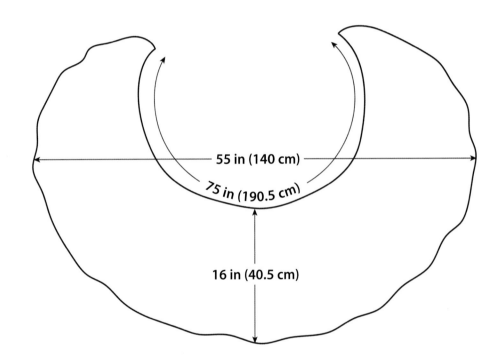

55 in (140 cm)

75 in (190.5 cm)

16 in (40.5 cm)

Iguazu Falls

It is amazing what you can do with a simple rectangle. In this book alone, I've made two ponchos from a rectangle in two different ways. Now, with the addition of armholes, a rectangle becomes an open front vest. Iguazu Falls starts with an intricate pattern at the bottom and then continues with an open mesh up the sides. Armholes are placed, and the back and fronts are worked separately for a bit. When the back and fronts are brought back together, lace worked across the top forms a draped collar and cascading fronts to finish your flowing garment.

Sizes: S (M, L, XL, 2XL)

Finished Measurements: *Total Width:* 44 (48.5, 53, 57.5, 62) in. [112 (123, 134.5, 146, 157.5) cm]; *Length:* 27 (28.25, 29.5, 30.75, 32) in. [68.5 (72, 75, 78, 81.5) cm]; *Armhole Depth:* 7 (7.5, 8, 8.5, 9) in. [18 (19, 20.5, 21.5, 23) cm]

To Fit: *Cross Back:* 14.5–15 (15.5–16, 16.5–17, 17.5, 18) in. [37–38 (39.5–40.5, 42–43, 44.5, 45.5) cm]; *Bust:* 32–34 (36–38, 40–42, 44–46, 48–50) in. [81–86 (91.5–96.5, 101.5–106.5, 111.5–117, 122–127) cm]

Yarn: Knit Picks Brava Bulky (100% premium acrylic; 136 yd./124 m; 3.53 oz./100 g); Wine, 4 (4, 5, 5, 6) skeins, approximately 420 (480, 550, 620, 690) yd. [384 (439, 503, 567, 631) m]

Needle: US size 13 (9 mm) 40–47 in. (100–120 cm) circular needle

Note: A circular needle is recommended to accommodate the large number of stitches; this piece is worked back and forth in rows.

Notions: Waste yarn, tapestry needle

Gauge: 10 sts and 14 rows = 4 in. (10 cm) in St st, blocked; 8 sts and 13 rows = 4 in. (10 cm) in Chart B Lace Pattern, blocked

Note

- Due to the size and complexity of the charts, this pattern does not include written instructions for the lace.

Instructions

Using the Knitted Cast-On method (see page 111), CO 98 (108, 118, 128, 138) sts.

BODY

Work Chart A Rows 1–26 once, working rep section 8 (9, 10, 11, 12) times.

Work Chart B Rows 1–4 twice, then work Rows 1 and 2 once more, working rep section 8 (9, 10, 11, 12) times.

Work Transition Chart Rows 1–6 once, working rep section 6 (7, 8, 9, 10) times.

Row 1 (RS): Work Right Edge Chart Row 1, pm, k68 (79, 88, 98, 108), pm, work Left Edge Chart Row 1.

Row 2 (WS): Work Left Edge Chart Row 2, sl m, purl to m, sl m, work Right Edge Chart Row 2.

Row 3: Work Right Edge Chart, sl m, knit to m, sl m, work Left Edge Chart.

Row 4: Work Left Edge Chart, sl m, purl to m, sl m, work Right Edge Chart.

Rep last 2 rows 0 (1, 2, 3, 4) more times.

You will have completed a total of 1 (1.5, 2, 2.5, 3) reps of Rows 1–4 of the combined Right/Left Edge Charts.

DIVIDE FOR BACK PANEL

With RS facing, place center 36 (38, 42, 44, 46) sts on waste yarn for Back Panel, and left 31 (35, 38, 42, 46) sts on waste yarn for Left Panel.

Chart A

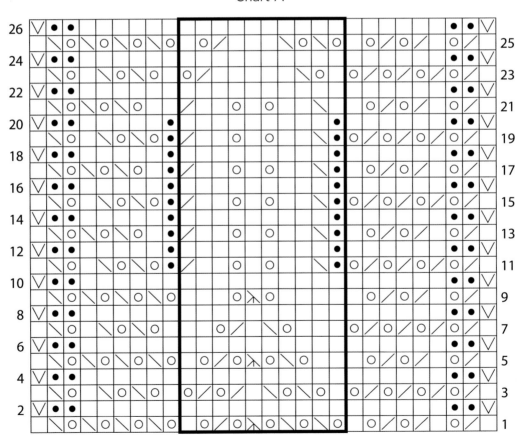

Repeat 8 (9, 10, 11, 12) times

Chart B

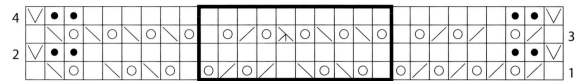

Repeat 8 (9, 10, 11, 12) times

Transition Chart

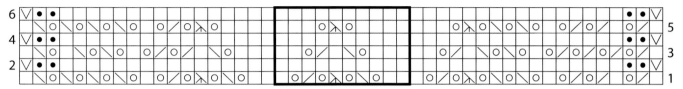

Repeat 6 (7, 8, 9, 10) times

Left Edge Chart

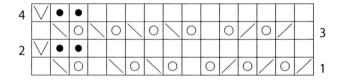

Right Edge Chart

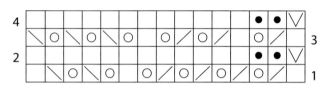

— Repeat	☐ YO
☐ RS: k; WS: p	╱ k2tog
• RS: p; WS: k	╲ ssk
∨ WS: s1 wyif	⋏ sl 1-k2tog-psso

RIGHT PANEL
Sizes S (L, 2XL) Only

Note: You will begin on Row 1 of Right Edge Chart.

Row 1 (RS): Work Right Edge Chart, sl m, k13 (20, 28) sts, YO, ssk, k1—31 (38, 46) sts.
Row 2 (WS): Sl 1 wyif, k2, purl to last 3 sts, k2, sl 1 wyif.

Rep last 2 rows 11 (13, 15) more times.

You will have completed a total of 6 (7, 8) reps of Rows 1–4 of Right Edge Chart.

Sizes M (XL) Only

Note: You will begin on Row 3 of Right Edge Chart.

Row 1 (RS): Work Right Edge Chart, sl m, k17 (24), YO, ssk, k1—35 (42) sts.
Row 2 (WS): Sl 1 wyif, k2, purl to last three sts, k2, sl 1 wyif.

Rep last 2 rows 12 (14) more times.

You will have completed a total of 6.5 (7.5) reps of Rows 1–4 of Right Edge Chart.

All Sizes
Transfer Right Panel sts to waste yarn.
Break yarn.

BACK PANEL
With RS facing, remount 36 (38, 42, 44, 46) Back Panel sts, and rejoin yarn.

Row 1 (RS): K1, k2tog, YO, k30 (32, 36, 38, 40) sts, YO, ssk, k1.
Row 2 (WS): Sl 1 wyif, k2, purl to last 3 sts, k2, sl 1 wyif.
Row 3: K1, k2tog, YO, knit to last 3 sts, YO, ssk, k1.
Row 4: Sl 1 wyif, k2, purl to last 3 sts, k2, sl 1 wyif.

Rep last 2 rows 10 (11, 12, 13, 14) more times.
Transfer Back Panel sts to waste yarn. Break yarn.

You will have worked a total of 24 (26, 28, 30, 32) rows.

LEFT PANEL
With RS facing, remount 31 (35, 38, 42, 46) Left Panel sts, and rejoin yarn.

Sizes S (L, 2XL) Only

Note: You will begin on Row 1 of Left Edge Chart.

Row 1 (RS): K1, k2tog, YO, knit to m, work Left Edge Chart—31 (38, 46) sts.
Row 2 (WS): Sl 1 wyif, k2, purl to last 3 sts, k2, sl 1 wyif.

Rep last 2 rows 11 (13, 15) more times.

You will have completed a total of 6 (7, 8) reps of Rows 1–4 of Left Edge Chart.

Sizes M (XL) Only

Note: You will begin on Row 3 of Left Edge Chart.

Row 1 (RS): K1, k2tog, YO, knit to m, work Left Edge Chart—35 (42) sts.
Row 2 (WS): Sl 1 wyif, k2, purl to last 3 sts, k2, sl 1 wyif.

Rep last 2 rows 12 (14) more times.

You will have completed a total of 6.5 (7.5) reps of Rows 1–4 of Left Edge Chart.

All Sizes
Do not cut yarn. Remount Back Panel and Right Panel sts onto the needle being careful not to twist.

JOIN

Note: On Row 1 you can cross the sts on either side of each join to neaten.

Row 1 (RS): Work Right Edge Chart, sl m, knit to m, sl m, work Left Edge Chart.

Row 2 (WS): Work Left Edge Chart, sl m, purl to m, sl m, work Right Edge Chart.

Rep last 2 rows once.

Work Chart B Rows 1–4 three times, working rep section 8 (9, 10, 11, 12) times.

Using the Very Stretchy Lace Bind-Off method (see page 112), BO all sts.

FINISHING

Weave in ends. Steam heat block to measurements. Trim ends.

Modify Me!

If you would want more volume around the neck and down the fronts, you can continue repeating Chart B until it is the depth you desire.

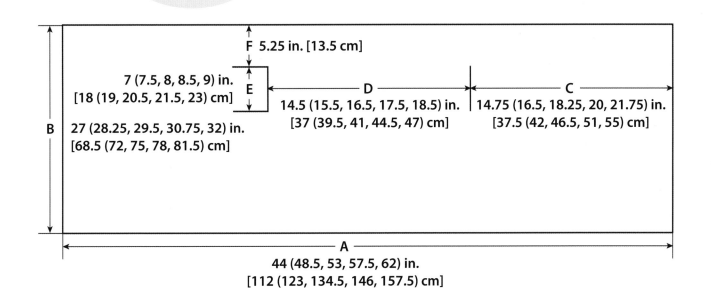

F 5.25 in. [13.5 cm]

7 (7.5, 8, 8.5, 9) in.
[18 (19, 20.5, 21.5, 23) cm]

E

D 14.5 (15.5, 16.5, 17.5, 18.5) in.
[37 (39.5, 41, 44.5, 47) cm]

C 14.75 (16.5, 18.25, 20, 21.75) in.
[37.5 (42, 46.5, 51, 55) cm]

27 (28.25, 29.5, 30.75, 32) in.
[68.5 (72, 75, 78, 81.5) cm]

B

A 44 (48.5, 53, 57.5, 62) in.
[112 (123, 134.5, 146, 157.5) cm]

Techniques

Knitting in the Round

There was a time where the only way to knit in the round was by using double-pointed needles (DPNs). It is a fine way of knitting in the round, and many knitters are devoted DPN users. But over the years innovations for knitting in the round have proliferated so that a knitter is spoiled for choice when it comes to options.

Circular needles are readily available and they can be used in many different ways. The knitter can match the circumference of the needle to the circumference of the project and simply knit away. There is also a widely used technique where the knitter uses two circular needles at a time. And a third option is to use an extra-long cable for the "magic loop" method. Personally, I am a devotee of the magic loop method, and all of the in-the-round projects in this book were knit in this manner.

In this book I have chosen not to specify an in-the-round technique. Each knitter should do what is most comfortable and produces an enjoyable knitting experience for them. For the patterns where the circumference of the piece decreases (such as the top of hats or those pesky thumbs), if you find it easier to switch from one method to another, or to pull out your DPNs, please do!

Cast-On/Bind-Off

There are many ways to begin and end your project. For each project in this book, I have chosen (and at times developed) the appropriate technique to meet the needs of the project. In the following pages you will find step-by-step instructions for all the cast-on and bind-off methods used in this book. I've even included a bonus joining technique that's used in Avasarala (page 89), the Kitchener stitch. For the particularly tricky steps, I've included photographs for clarification.

Cast-Ons

CABLE CAST-ON

Set-Up: Make a slipknot, leaving a long tail for weaving in later; place slipknot on LH needle—this counts as your first st.

1. Insert RH needle into st on LH needle kwise, wrap working yarn around RH needle, and pull through new st.
2. Place new st on LH needle (without twisting) and tighten—1 st created.
3. Insert RH needle between the first and second sts on LH needle from front to back, wrap working yarn around RH needle, and pull through new st.
4. Place new st on LH needle pwise and tighten—1 st created.

Rep Steps 3 and 4 until you have cast on desired number of sts.

CIRCULAR CAST-ON

Set-Up: Create a loop with your yarn with the working yarn up, the tail down, and the loop to the left of the crossing point as shown. The working yarn will lie on top of the tail end. Pinch the crossing point between your thumb and 4th finger, tensioning the working yarn with your index and middle fingers.

1. Insert needle into the loop and behind the working yarn from right to left, pull working yarn through the loop—1 st created.

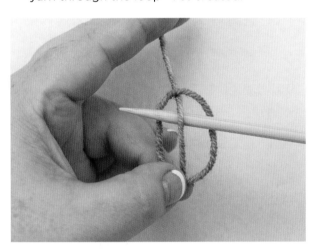

2. Without going through the loop, put the needle behind the working yarn from right to left like a YO (2nd st formed with YO)—1 st created.

Rep Steps 1 and 2 until you have cast on desired number of sts; shown here with 5 sts cast on.

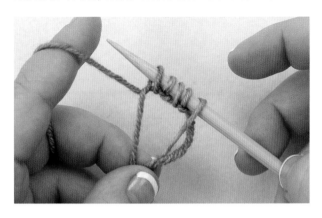

Finally: Position sts for preferred method of knitting in the rnd. After you have completed a few rnds pull on tail to cinch the sts and close the hole.

Note: If casting on an even number of sts, the last st will be a YO and can be added just before starting your first round.

KNITTED CAST-ON

Set-Up: Make a slipknot, leaving a long tail for weaving in later; place slipknot on LH needle—this counts as your first st.

1. Insert RH needle into st on LH needle kwise, wrap working yarn around RH needle, and pull through new st.

2. Place new st on LH needle pwise (without twisting) and tighten—1 st created.

Rep Steps 1 and 2 until you have cast on desired number of sts.

LONG TAIL CAST-ON

Set-Up 1: Make a slipknot, leaving a tail three times the length of your desired cast-on and place slipknot on RH needle—counts as your first st.

Set-Up 2: Keep the slipknot from slipping off the needle by placing your right index finger on top of it. Hold yarn in your left hand with working yarn running over your index finger and tail yarn running over your thumb.

Set-Up 3: Hold both ends in the palm of your hand, grasping them with remaining three fingers; it will look similar to holding a slingshot.

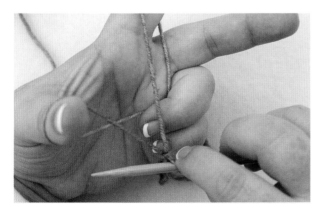

1. Bring needle tip down beneath the left-most strand held around the thumb and up between the two strands looping the thumb.

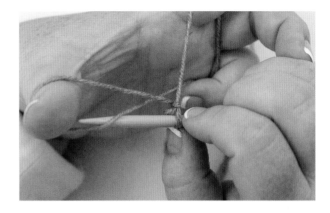

2. Take the needle over the right-most strand around the thumb, over and behind the left-most strand of yarn around your index finger; bring the tip of the needle down between the two strands looping your index finger.

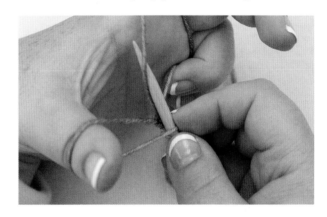

3. Pull this left-most strand on your index finger through the loop you've made on your thumb, taking it back through the path you just made. Remove your thumb from the tail loop of yarn, lifting it up and over the needle.

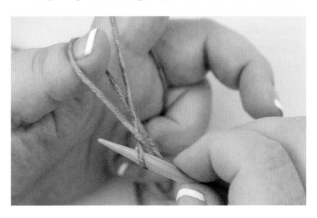

4. Move your thumb back under the loose tail of yarn to tighten the st and return to the starting slingshot position—1 st created.

Rep Steps 1–4 until you have cast on desired number of sts.

Bind-Offs

1X1 RIBBING BIND-OFF
(first stitch to be bound off is a purl)
Set-Up: P1.
  1. K1.
  2. Insert LH needle through front loops of last 2 sts on RH needle and k2tog tbl—1 st bound off.
  3. P1.
  4. Insert LH needle through back loops of last 2 sts on RH needle and p2tog—1 st bound off.
Rep Steps 1–4 until all sts are bound off.

1X1 RIBBING BIND-OFF
(first stitch to be bound off is a knit)
Set-Up: K1.
  1. P1.
  2. Insert LH needle through back loops of last 2 sts on RH needle and p2tog—1 st bound off.
  3. K1.
  4. Insert LH needle through front loops of last 2 sts on RH needle and k2tog tbl—1 st bound off.
Rep Steps 1–4 until all sts are bound off.

EXPANDABLE LACE BIND-OFF, KNIT VARIANT
Set-Up: Sl 1 pwise wyib.
  1. K1.
  2. Insert LH needle through front loops of last 2 sts on RH needle and k2tog tbl—1 st bound off.
Rep Steps 1 and 2 until all sts are bound off.

EXPANDABLE LACE BIND-OFF, PURL VARIANT
Set-Up: Sl 1 pwise wyib.
  1. P1.
  2. Insert LH needle through back loops of last 2 sts on RH needle and p2tog—1 st bound off.
Rep Steps 1 and 2 until all sts are bound off.

VERY STRETCHY LACE BIND-OFF
Set-Up: K1.
  1. YO, k1. [3 sts on RH needle]
  2. Insert the LH needle through the front legs of the last 2 sts on RH needle and k2tog tbl. [2 sts on RH needle]
  3. Lift the right-most st on the RH needle up, over, and off the tip of the needle—1 st bound off.
Rep Steps 1–3 until 1 st remains on LH needle. Sl last st from RH to LH needle pwise and k2tog tbl.

Kitchener Stitch

Hold needles with live sts parallel to each other with points to the right and the working yarn coming off the back needle.

Set-Up: Insert yarn needle pwise into the first st on the front needle and then insert yarn needle kwise into the first st on the back needle and pull through yarn. Both sts remain on the needles.

1. Insert yarn needle kwise into the first st on the front needle and pull the yarn though, dropping st from knitting needle.

2. Insert yarn needle pwise into the next st on the front needle and pull the yarn through, st remains on the needle.

3. Insert yarn needle pwise into the first st on the back needle and pull the yarn through, dropping st from knitting needle.

4. Insert yarn needle kwise into the next st on the back needle and pull the yarn through, st remains on the needle.

Repeat Steps 1–4, tightening yarn as needed as you progress, to the last 2 sts, one on each needle; then work Step 1, followed by Step 3.

⚭ ABBREVIATIONS ⚭

Instructions following an * or within ( ) or [ ] are to be repeated the number of times indicated.

BO	Bind off as instructed in each pattern.
CDD	Central double decrease; slip two stitches as if to k2tog, knit next stitch, and pass both slipped stitches over together. Two stitches decreased.
CO	Cast on as instructed in each pattern.
dec('d)	Decrease(d)
EOR	End of round
inc('d)	Increase(d)
k	Knit; move the yarn to the back of the work between the needles, insert right-hand needle from left to right through front loop of next stitch on left-hand needle, wrap yarn around right-hand needle and pull through stitch.
k1fb	Knit one front and back; knit into the front loop of the next stitch as usual but leave it on the needle, then knit into the back loop of the same stitch. One stitch increased.
k1 tbl	Knit one through the back loop; insert right-hand needle from right to left through the back loop of the next stitch on the left-hand needle and knit. This creates a twisted stitch.
k2tog	Knit two stitches together as one; insert right-hand needle from left to right through the front loops of next two stitches on the left-hand needle and knit them as if they were one stitch. One stitch decreased.
k2tog tbl	Knit two stitches together through the back loops as one; insert right-hand needle from right to left through the back loops of the next two stitches on the left-hand needle and knit them as if they were one stitch. One stitch decreased.
kwise	Knitwise; as to knit

kYOk	Knit, yarn over, knit; knit into the front loop of next stitch as usual but leave it on the needle, YO, then knit into the same stitch again. Two stitches increased.
LH	Left-hand
m	Marker
M1L	Make one left; using the left needle, pick up the strand of yarn that runs between the last stitch worked and the next stitch to be worked from front to back, then knit this strand through the back loop. One stitch increased.
M1R	Make one right; using the left needle, pick up the strand of yarn that runs between the last stitch worked and the next stitch to be worked from back to front, and knit this strand through the front loop. One stitch increased.
M1PR	Make one purl right; using the left needle, pick up the strand of yarn that runs between the last stitch worked and the next stitch to be worked from back to front, and purl this strand through the front loop. One stitch increased.
p	Purl; move yarn to the front of the work between the needles, insert right-hand needle from right to left through front loop of next stitch on left-hand needle, wrap yarn around right-hand needle and pull through stitch.
p2tog	Purl two stitches together as one; insert right-hand needle from right to left through the front loops of next two stitches on the left-hand needle and purl them as if they were one stitch. One stitch decreased.
p3tog	Purl three stitches together as one; insert right-hand needle from right to left through the front loops of next three stitches on the left-hand needle and purl them as if they were one stitch. Two stitches decreased.
pm	Place marker
pwise	Purlwise; as to purl
rep	Repeat
RH	Right-hand
rnd(s)	Round(s)
rm	Remove marker
RS	Right side
sl 1-k2tog-psso	Slip one, knit two together, pass slipped stitch over; slip one stitch as to knit, knit the next two stitches together as one, insert left-hand needle into the front loop of the slipped stitch from left to right and pass it over the k2tog stitch and drop it off the needle. Two stitches decreased.

sl 1-k2-psso	Slip one, knit two, pass slipped stitch over; slip one stitch as to knit, knit the next two stitches, insert left-hand needle into the front loop of the slipped stitch from left to right and pass it over the two knit stitches and drop it off the needle. One stitch decreased.
skp	Slip one, knit one, pass slipped stitch over; slip one stitch as to knit, knit next stitch, insert left-hand needle into the front loop of the slipped stitch from left to right and pass it over the knit stitch and drop it off the needle. One stitch decreased.
sl 1	Slip; with yarn held to wrong side of knitting unless otherwise indicated, insert right-hand needle into front loop of next stitch on left-hand needle from right to left, transfer stitch to right-hand needle without working stitch.
sl m	Slip marker; insert right-hand needle into marker on left-hand needle, transfer marker to right-hand needle.
ssk	Slip, slip, knit; slip next two stitches on left-hand needle individually as to knit, return them to left-hand needle purlwise and knit them together through their back loops. One stitch decreased.
ssk-pssf-sl 1	Slip, slip, knit, pass slipped stitch forward, slip; ssk, then return new stitch to left-hand needle, pass the second stitch on left-hand needle over the ssk stitch and off the needle, slip ssk stitch purlwise back to right-hand needle. Two stitches decreased.
st(s)	Stitch(es)
St st	Stockinette stitch
WS	Wrong side
wyib	With yarn in back
wyif	With yarn in front
YO	Yarn over; bring yarn forward and over right-hand needle to create new stitch (see page 3 for more details on working yarn overs). One stitch increased.

❍❍❍ YARN SOURCES ❍❍❍

Anzula Luxury Fibers
www.anzula.com

Berroco, Inc.
www.berroco.com

Blue Sky Fibers (Spud &
Chloë)
www.blueskyfibers.com

Cascade Yarns
www.cascadeyarns.com

Knit Picks
www.knitpicks.com

Lion Brand Yarn
www.lionbrand.com

Malabrigo
www.malabrigoyarn.com

Miss Babs Hand-Dyed Yarns
& Fibers
www.missbabs.com

MollyGirl Yarn
www.mollygirlyarn.com

Stitch Sprouts
www.stitchsprouts.com

Patons Yarn / Bernat Yarn
www.yarnspirations.com

Plymouth Yarn
www.plymouthyarn.com

⚭ ACKNOWLEDGMENTS ⚭

It may be my name on the cover, but it took the hands and minds of many people to make this book a reality and I would like to take a moment to acknowledge them.

Technical editors are indispensable in ensuring that the patterns are accurate and free of errors. My thanks to Heather Zoppetti for her services in this area.

It took a lot of knitting to make all of the samples in this book come to life, and I thank Kelly Yangula Asfour for being my extra pair of capable hands.

No one would even consider knitting one of these patterns if it were not for the beautiful photographs taken by the talented Gale Zucker. Thank you for using your vision to uplift mine. And, of course, it took amazing models to make my pieces come to life. They are Ariana McLean Hernandez, Yliana Tibitoski, Rachel Toussaint, and Doug Toussaint.

To Roger and Elliott: With my first book you supported me unfailingly, but this time you knew what you were getting into and you let me do it anyway. You are my best guys. I love you both.

⊙⊙ VISUAL INDEX ⊙⊙

Shoot the Moon 9

Asymmetrical
Balance 13

Sparrow Grass
Hat 17

Rocinante 23

Coefficient of
Modulation 27

To Warmly Go 31

Giant Elves 37

Teeter Totter
Toque 41

Cinches and
Ladders 45

Signet Throw 49

Dash Panel 55

Un, Deux, Trois 59

Bonus Stitch
Hat 65

Drunk Spider 69

Shorty Squiggle
Mitts 73

Hearts in Chains
Poncho 77

Rupee Slouch 83

Avasarala 89

Bitis Shawl 95

Iguazu Falls 101